Principles of Strategic Data Science

Creating value from data, big and small

Dr Peter Prevos

Principles of Strategic Data Science

Author: Dr Peter Prevos

Managing Editor: Aditya Shah

Acquisitions Editor: Bridget Neale

Production Editor: Nitesh Thakur

Editorial Board: David Barnes, Mayank Bhardwaj, Ewan Buckingham, Simon Cox, Mahesh Dhyani, Taabish Khan, Manasa Kumar, Alex Mazonowicz, Douglas Paterson, Dominic Pereira, Shiny Poojary, Erol Staveley, Ankita Thakur, and Jonathan Wray

First Published: May 2019

Production Reference: 2270819

ISBN: 978-1-83898-529-5

Published by Packt Publishing Ltd.

Livery Place, 35 Livery Street

Birmingham B3 2PB, UK

Table of Contents

Preface

About the Book

Principles of Data Science is created to help you join the dots between mathematics, programming, and business analysis.

I am not a data scientist. These might be strange words to read in a book about data science, so please allow me to explain. This book is the result of a 25-year career in civil engineering, building and managing structures in Europe, Africa, Asia, and Australia. Most of my tasks involve managing and analyzing large amounts of data. Cost estimates, volume calculations, modelling river flows, structural calculations, Monte Carlo simulations, and many other types of number crunching are integral to my work as an engineer.

My journey toward what we now call data science started at university. When studying engineering in the Netherlands, I wrote computer code in the Pascal and BASIC languages. I loved spending time in the computer lab and writing software to solve technical problems. The dean advised me to switch from civil engineering to computer science, but I enjoyed writing software to solve engineering problems, not for the sake of it, so I did not heed the advice.

In my first job as a civil engineer, my company introduced the now defunct *Lotus 123* spreadsheet. When first using that package, I thought it was the best thing since sliced bread. Graphical output and managing data were complex tasks when writing code in those days. The allure of the spreadsheet was the ability to combine input with computer code and show the results in text or graphs, all in one convenient file.

Over the following two decades, I wrote hundreds of spreadsheets to solve a myriad of engineering problems. I even developed a 'jungle' of interconnected spreadsheets to manage the logistics of a large river engineering project in Bangladesh. The complexity of this task took me beyond the limits of what spreadsheets can achieve. Throughout my career, I have had many nightmarish experiences, trying to reverse-engineer spreadsheets to figure out how they work – even ones I wrote myself. The combination of data, code, and output that I loved at the start of my career became a source of frustration.

My love affair with the venerable spreadsheet ended when writing my doctoral dissertation. Excel was incapable of helping me with complex statistics such as structural equation modelling or network analysis. A colleague suggested looking into this new thing called 'data science.' I decided to learn how to write code in R, a specialized computer language for statistical analysis. The R language is like a Swiss Army chainsaw for engineers, with capabilities that far exceed anything a spreadsheet can do.

I now manage the data science function for a water utility in regional Australia. Through my experience with practical data analysis and expertise in management, I have developed a strategic approach to data science. I have published and presented my views on strategic data science at conferences in Australia and New Zealand. This book is an expanded version of an article I wrote for the journal of the Australian Water Association, which became one of the most downloaded papers. *Lifting the Big Data Veil* describes a back-to-basics approach to how to maximize the value we can extract from data assets. This book dives deeper into the principles of data science first presented in this paper.

I have written this book from the perspective of an engineer and a social scientist, but the same principles are valid for any field of human endeavor. All professionals and scientists rely on data to make decisions. Data science provides a systematic approach to making better business decisions and discovering new patterns in society or nature.

My approach in this book goes back to the basics of what it means to create value from data. This book is not a treatise on machine learning, mathematics, or developing software, but a practical guide to strategically and systematically using data to create a better world. This book is pragmatic because it doesn't dwell on the future promises of machine learning, artificial intelligence, or quantum computing. The framework in this book is inspired by my current and desired practice as an engineer and social scientist, with a data science responsibility and best-practice in management.

About the Author

Dr Peter Prevos is a civil engineer and social scientist who also dabbles in theatrical magic. Peter has almost three decades of experience as a water engineer and manager, working in Europe, Africa, Asia, and Australia. He has worked on marine engineering, drinking water, and sewage treatment projects. Throughout his career, analysing data has been a central theme.

He also has a PhD in marketing and is the author of Customer Experience Management for Water Utilities. In his work, he aims to combine the social sciences with engineering to create value for customers. Peter occasionally lectures marketing for MBA students.

He is currently responsible for developing and implementing the data science strategy for a water utility in regional Australia. The objective of this strategy is to create value from data through useful, sound, and aesthetic data science. His mission is to breed unicorn data scientists by motivating other water professionals to ditch their spreadsheets and learn how to write code.

Learning Objectives

- Get familiar with the five most important steps of data science
- Use the Conway diagram to visualize the technical skills of the data science team
- Understand the limitations of data science from a mathematical and ethical perspective
- Get a quick overview of machine learning
- Gain insight into the purpose of using data science in your work
- Understand the role of data science managers and expectations from them

Approach

This book covers the basic approach of creating value from data. It is developed as a practical guide to strategically and systematically use data to create a better world. It doesn't dwell on promises of machine learning, artificial intelligence or quantum computing. The framework in this book is inspired by the author's current and desired practice as an engineer and social scientist, with a data science responsibility and best-practice in management.

Audience

This book is ideal for data scientists and data analysts who are looking for a practical guide to strategically and systematically use data. This book is also useful for those who want to understand in detail what is data science and how can an organization take the data-driven approach. Prior programming knowledge of Python and R is assumed.

Preface to Second Edition

The second edition of this book contains many grammar fixes. Thanks to David Smith and Catherine Cousins for spotting these mistakes.

Interestingly, the machine learning program I used for checking the text did not identify many of these mistakes in the first version. This experience strengthens one of the points in this book, which is that artificial intelligence is not a replacement for natural intelligence.

Acknowledgements

My career has been dynamic and varied but analyzing data has been the one constant in my career. My toolkit to convert data to actionable intelligence has evolved significantly over the past twenty-five years. My former and current colleagues helped me to accumulate new approaches and skills, which led me to write this book.

In my first job as an engineer, Wim van Vliet in Johannesburg was a significant influence on my development as an engineer. Through him, I learned how to convert my theoretical knowledge into a systematic approach to solving real problems.

René Zekveld was my manager at Boskalis when I worked on marine engineering projects in Hong Kong and Bangladesh. René taught me tricks of the trade on how to interpret data to achieve sound business outcomes. He emphasized the importance of the relationship between reality and data. Our long discussions about data showed me that actionable intelligence and insight are essential outcomes.

After my international career, I moved back to the Netherlands and spent time with Rijkswaterstaat, the government agency responsible for keeping the country from flooding. Working for this organization exposed me to probabilistic approaches in cost estimation and project management. We regularly worked with mathematicians, whose names are lost in time, to help us grasp the complexity of our analysis. Working for this organization advanced my skills in using mathematics to create value from data.

At the start of the new millennium, I started my current job at Coliban Water, a water utility in regional Australia. Brad Dole, a former IT manager, has been influential in how I now work with data. As an IT manager, Brad provided me with the freedom to maximize the capabilities of the company hardware. Brad also has a razor-sharp insight into data and how to convert business problems into code. Under Brad's guidance, we developed several in-house software solutions, which took my software development skills beyond a mere hobby.

Jenny Fogarty is my current colleague and the data architect at Coliban Water. We have worked on developing software and reporting mechanisms for many years. Through her expertise, I learned everything I know about managing data. It was on her advice five years ago that I started researching the topic of data science. Not only has her advice helped me to complete my dissertation about customer centricity, but it has also transformed the way I view my profession.

No vision of data science can ever be implemented without people doing the work. Gary Schurr has over the past few years been great at finding innovative ways to report information. His critical helps to straighten out some of my more impulsive ideas.

I started my formal journey into data science by doing a range of courses on the Coursera website. The data science specialization by John Hopkins University taught me the principles of how to use the R language for statistical computing. The inspiring lectures by Roger Peng, Jeff Leek and Brian Caffo helped me to think more systematically in how I deal with data.

My manager David Sheehan often encourages me to develop new ideas and 'conquer the world'. This book is just another small step in that direction. It would not have existed without the freedom David provides me to shape the data science function at Coliban Water and the broader water industry in Australia.

Lastly, I thank all my colleagues at Coliban Water and the broader Australian water industry who indulge me in my geekiness and enthusiasm to find data solutions to improve the way we service our customers. This book is the direct result of the positive feedback from the people that have attended my conference presentations and read my publications and articles on my Lucid Manager–https://lucidmanager.org website.

1

What is Data Science?

Introduction

The activity of analyzing data is as old as human culture. The earliest known form of writing is not an epic poem or religious text, but data. The Ishango bone is an engraved fibula of a baboon which was carved in central Africa 20,000 years ago. Some scholars hypothesized that the carvings represent an early number system, as it lists several prime numbers, while others believe it to be a calendar. Some researchers dismiss these ideas and believe the markings merely improve grip when using the bone as a club. Whatever their purpose, the groupings of the markings are distinctly mathematical, as shown in the *Figure 1.1 (Pletser, V. (2012). Does the Ishango Bone Indicate Knowledge of the Base 12? An Interpretation of a Prehistoric Discovery, the First Mathematical Tool of Humankind. Eprint—*https://arxiv.org/abs/1204.1019*)*

The following image shows the markings on the Ishango Bone:

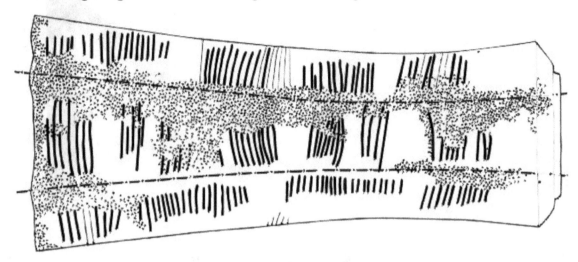

Figure 1.1: Markings on the Ishango Bone

Ancient cultures around the world collected data by observing nature and the stars to predict when they needed to move camp, start sowing crops, hunt seasonal animals, and to obtain whatever other knowledge they required for survival. These proto-scientific methods were the first attempts at science, as these early researchers collected data to explain the world in logical terms. These primitive forms of science helped these people to understand their world and control their destiny, which is precisely what contemporary science seeks to achieve.

Mathematics was an integral part of ancient civilizations. Sumeria, Egypt, Rome, and other advanced ancient civilizations used mathematics to manage their society and build their elaborate cities. The origins of civilization as we now know it lies in Mesopotamia, current-day Iraq. Archaeologists have excavated thousands of clay tablets that record their day-to-day activities such as land sales, delivery of goods, and other commercial transactions. Around that same time in Pharaonic Egypt, the first census took place, recording demographic data about its inhabitants. (*Kelleher, J.D., & Tierney, B. (2018). Data science. Cambridge, Massachusetts: The MIT Press*) These examples show that collecting data and using it to control and improve our world is an ancient human activity.

This time was also a period of the first significant mathematical discoveries and inventions. Mathematics was, however, more than a language to model the world. To the great Ancient Greek mathematician Pythagoras, numbers possessed meaning beyond their ability to describe quantity. In these early days of intellectual exploration, divination was the most popular method to predict the future. Astrologers mapped the skies or studied the entrails of a bird to find a relationship between these patterns and their world. In these divination systems, mathematics was practiced as a tool to manage society through engineering and bookkeeping, not as a tool to describe the world.

The scientific revolution of the seventeenth century replaced divination with a mathematical approach to understanding the world. Since the work of René Descartes, mathematics has taken the form of a method to describe the world and to predict its future. (*Davis, P.J., & Hersh, R. (1990). Descartes' Dream. The World According to Mathematics London: Penguin*) This revolution in how we perceive the world mathematically is what enabled the industrial revolution. Early technology enhanced our physical capabilities with machines, while modern technology improves our minds with computers. Machines make us stronger and faster, and their development revolutionized society during the first industrial revolution. Computers enhance aspects of our mental abilities, and we are in the middle of a second industrial revolution, which is not fueled by oil and coal, but by data.

The idea that data can be used to understand the world is thus almost as old as humanity itself and has gradually evolved into what we now call data science. We can use some basic data science to review the development of this term over time.

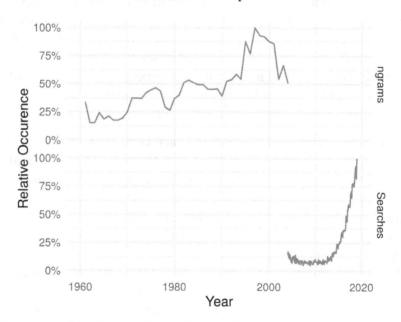

Figure 1.2: Frequency of the bi-gram 'data science' in literature and Google searches occurrence ordered as per highest percentage

The combination of the words data and science might seem relatively new, but the Google **N-gram Viewer** shows that this **bi-gram** has been in use since the middle of the last century. An n-gram is a sequence of words, with a bi-gram being any combination of two words. Google's n-gram viewer is a searchable database of millions of scanned books published before 2008. This database is a source for predictive text algorithms, as it contains a fantastic amount of knowledge about how people use various languages. (*Google Books Ngram Viewer*—https://books. google.com/ngrams/graph?content=data+science&year_start=1900&year_ end=2008&corpus=15&smoothing=3&share=&direct_url=t1%3B%2Cdata%20 science%3B%2Cc0 *Retrieved 25 January* 2019)

The n-gram database shows that the term data science emerged in the middle of the last century, when electronic computation became a topic of study. In those days, the discipline was a science about storing and manipulating data. The current definition has drifted away from this initial academic activity to a business activity.

Judging by another Google database, data science started its journey from obscurity to becoming the latest business fad only a few years ago. The `Google Trends` database shows the frequency of search terms over time. Google Trends reveals a steady increase in the popularity of data science as a search term, starting in 2013. (*Google Trends*— https://trends.google.com/trends/explore?date=all&q=data%20science *Retrieved* 25 *January* 2019)

Figure 1.2 visualizes these two trends. The horizontal axis shows the years from 1960 until recently. The vertical axis shows the relative number of occurrences compared to the maximum, which is how Google reports search numbers. In an absolute sense, the number of occurrences in books was much lower than current search volumes. While the increase in attention has steeply risen since 2012, the term started its journey toward being a business buzzword in the 1960s. Although we can speak of the recent hype, the use of the bi-gram data science shows a slow evolution, with a recent spike in interest.

The expectations of the benefits of data science are very high. Business authors position data science and its natural partner, 'big data', as a panacea for all societal problems and a means to increase business profits. (*Clegg, B.* (2017). *Big Data: How the Information Revolution Is Transforming Our Lives. Icon Books*). In a 2012 article in Harvard Business Review, Davenport and Patil even proclaimed the role of data scientist as the "sexiest job of the 21st century". (*Davenport, T.H., & Patil, D.J.* (2012). *Data scientist: The sexiest job of the 21st century*—https://hbr.org/2012/10/data-scientist-the-sexiest-job-of-the-21st-century *Harvard Business Review*, 90(10), 70–76) Who would not want to be part of a new profession with such enticing career prospects? It is not a stretch to hypothesize that their article was one of the causes of the increased search volume reported by Google.

The recent popularity of data science as a business activity suggests that it is just a fancy way of saying business analysis. In my talks about data science in Australia and New Zealand, I regularly meet fellow managers who are skeptical about the proclaimed wizard-like abilities of data scientists and the unbounded promises of machine learning. Much of the data science promise relates to the success stories of internet corporations such as Google and Facebook and many other smaller players in the digital economy. For these organizations, data science is a core competency, as their value proposition is centered around data.

For organizations that deliver physical products or non-digital services, data science is about improving how they collect, store, and analyze data to extract more value from this resource. The objective of data science is not the data itself but is closely intertwined with the strategic goals of the organization. These objectives broadly range from increasing the return to shareholders to providing benefit to society overall. Whatever the kind of organization you are in, the purpose of data science is to assist managers to change reality into a more desirable state. A data scientist achieves this by measuring the current and past states of reality and using mathematical tools to predict a future state.

The term data science is unfortunate in the way it is now used, because it is paradoxically not a science of data. A data scientist is not somebody who researches the properties of data. Other definitions see data scientists as mathematicians and computer scientists that invent new ways of analyzing data. More commonly, data science is closely related to business outcomes.

Data science is a systematic and strategic approach to using data to solve practical problems. The problems of the data scientist are practical because pure science has a different objective to business. A data scientist in an organization is less interested in a generalized solution to a problem and focuses on improving how the organization achieves its goals. Perhaps the combination of the words data and science should be reserved for academics.

There are some signals that the excitement of the past few years is waning. Data science blogger Matt Tucker has declared the death of the data scientist. (*Tucker, M. (2018). The Death of the Data Scientist. Retrieved 9 February 2019 from Data Science Central*–https://www.datasciencecentral.com/profiles/blogs/the-death-of-the-data-scientist) For many business problems, the hardcore methods of machine learning result in over-analyzing the issue. Tucker provides an anecdote of a group of data scientists who spent a lot of time fine-tuning a complex neural network. The data scientists gave up when a young graduate with expertise in the subject matter used a linear regression that was more accurate than their neural network.

The negative chatter on the internet about data science as a business discipline might imply that the hype is receding. We should, however, not throw the baby out with the bathwater. The recent interest in analyzing data has raised the stakes in how organizations use this valuable resource. Even after the inflated expectations recede, data science as a profession has a useful contribution to make. All data, big and small, is a resource to improve how organizations perform.

This book looks at data science as the strategic and systematic approach to the fine art of analyzing data to solve business problems. This conceptualization of data science is not a complete definition. Computational analysis of data is also practiced as a science and as a scientific method for research in many areas. This book is written from a business perspective, and these other uses on data science are not further considered.

Data-Driven Organization

The previous section showed that data science is not necessarily just hype, but a strategic and systematic approach to using data. Using data in organizations is also called business analytics or evidence-based management. There are also specific approaches, such as **Six-Sigma**, that use statistical analysis to improve business processes. Many advocates of data science claim that the old and new approaches are different. Most definitions of data science focus on pattern recognition using large sets of data through machine learning. (*Kelleher & Tierney (2018)*). How does data science relate to its predecessor buzzwords? To understand this difference, we need to explore the early history of using data in business.

The idea that management can be science is just over a century old. Frederick Taylor was an American engineer who was dissatisfied with how factories were managed. He was a hands-on engineer who spent much time on the factory floor. Taylor noticed how workers used rules of thumb, instead of analyzing problems systematically. He writes, in *The Principles of Scientific Management (1911)*, how he improved the process of manually loading massive lumps of iron at the Midvale Steel Company by measuring processes and analyzing the data. (*Taylor, F.W. (1997). The Principles of Scientific Management. Mineola, N.Y: Dover Publications*)

Although Taylor revolutionized the way we manage organizations, he despised laborers. Taylor believed that it "would be possible to train an intelligent gorilla to become more efficient" than a factory worker. His quest for scientific management was driven by an urge to remove power from the workforce and look at business processes in an abstract mathematical sense. His work was controversial in his own time, as it was the subject of a formal government inquiry. This background about Taylor is not just a bit of trivia, but a valuable lesson about ensuring to include a human dimension in what we analyze. The positive legacy of Taylor is that he planted the seed for a scientific approach to managing an organization. All methods share his ideal of using data to prevent biases in management.

Managers are faced with deciding what to do next in uncertain environments and often use their experience and intuition to determine the next course of action, instead of data and logic. While experience and intuition are highly valuable, our minds are prone to biases and non-rational thinking. Our rationality is not unlimited but is bounded by factors outside of our control. The amount of information, the time available to solve a problem, and our mental capacity are all limited. Our brains are wired to quickly recognize patterns in nature because it helps us in our daily lives. Mental shortcuts, the rules of thumb despised by Taylor, help us to make fast decisions in emergencies, but they can also lead to sub-optimal outcomes.

The world of business is not something we have necessarily evolved to navigate, and we are thus not very good at interpreting large amounts of abstract data. Because our minds are programmed to recognize patterns, we often see regularities where there are none, which psychologists call pareidolia. This condition causes us to recognize animals in clouds or see the image of Jesus in a piece of toast, or a face on the surface of Mars. Pareidolia serves us well because it enables graphical communication, but it becomes a hindrance when analyzing large sets of data. Interestingly, neural networks can also be trained to experience pareidolia. When manipulating the settings of image-recognition software, computers can be taught to recognize images in random data and effectively hallucinate a new reality. (*Mordvintsev, A., Olah, C. & Tyka, M. (2015). Inceptionism—* http://ai.googleblog.com/2015/06/inceptionism-going-deeper-into-neural.html: *Going Deeper into Neural Networks. Retrieved 15 February 2019*)

Besides inherent biases through the limits of our rationality, social circumstances can also prevent us from optimizing decisions. Groupthink and office politics are often strong drivers of decisions in organizations. Social belonging is a strong motivator for our behavior and is one of the major driving forces behind advertising. Asch's conformity experiment illustrates how strong these social biases can be. Solomon Asch demonstrated that even when people are fully aware of the rational answer to a simple question, they will in most instances yield their opinion to match that of the group, even when it is clearly the wrong choice. (*Asch Conformity Experiment (YouTube—* https://www.youtube.com/watch?v=TYIh4MkcfJA). *Downloaded 14 February 2019*)

One of the greatest revolutions in human thinking is the 15th-century Copernican twist. From our limited perspective, the earth seems flat and the sun and moon revolve around us. When Copernicus looked through a telescope to amplify his naked-eye observations, a new reality emerged, and with it, a better model of our solar system. What we learned from Copernicus is that we need to enhance our perception and thinking skills with technology to draw correct conclusions. Data science is to business what the telescope is to astronomy. Sound analysis of data helps us to remove our natural biases and replace our rules of thumb with logic.

Just like a long-enough lever can make us physically strong enough to lift the world, the tools of data science make us mentally stronger in understanding and controlling the world. While the uncertainties of the realities of business can never be eliminated, evidence-based management ensures that managers make decisions based on the best available data. Data science is the toolkit that assists managers to base their decisions on evidence. Using the principles of data science will improve the way managers decide between alternative courses of action.

Using a scientific approach to data is, however, not a simple road to success. Data science is a human activity that encompasses all the biases and limitations. The results of data science are also not ethically neutral and require a moral perspective to ensure that no harm is done. The key to minimizing these biases is to use a systematic approach.

The Data Revolution

Since Taylor's first writings, businesses and non-profit organizations have sought to become driven by evidence to reduce unconscious bias in their decisions. Although data science is merely a new term for something that has existed for decades, some recent developments have created a watershed between the old and new ways of doing business. The difference between traditional business analysis and the new world of data science is threefold.

Firstly, businesses have much more data available than ever before. The move to electronic transactions means that almost every process leaves a digital footprint. Collecting and storing this data has become exponentially cheaper than in the days of pencil and paper. Many organizations collect this data without maximizing the value they extract from it. After the data is used for its intended purpose, it becomes 'dark data', stored on servers but languishing in obscurity. This data provides opportunities to optimize how an organization operates by recycling and analyzing it to learn about the past to create a better future.

Secondly, the computing power that is now available in a tablet was not long ago the domain of supercomputers. Piotr Luszczek showed that an iPad 2 matches the performance of the world's fastest computer in 1985. (*Larabel, M. (2012). Apple iPad 2 As Fast As The Cray-2 Supercomputer. Retrieved 4 February 2019 from (Phoronix—*https://www.phoronix.com/scan.php?page=news_item&px=MTE4NjU*))* The affordability of vast computing power enables even small organizations to reap the benefits of advanced analytics.

Lastly, complex machine learning algorithms are freely available as open source software, and a laptop is all that is needed to implement sophisticated mathematical analyses. The R language for statistical computing, and Python, are both potent tools that can undertake a vast array of data science tasks such as complex visualizations and machine learning. These languages are 'Swiss army chainsaws' that can tackle any business analysis problem. Part of their power lies in the healthy communities that support each other in their journey to mastering these languages.

These three changes have caused a revolution in how we create value from data. The barriers to entry for even small organizations to leverage information technology are very low. The only hurdle is to make sense of the fast-moving developments and follow a strategic approach instead of chasing the hype.

This revolution is not necessarily only about powerful machine learning algorithms, but about a more scientific way of solving business problems. The definition of data science in this book is not restricted to machine learning, big data, and artificial intelligence. These developments are essential aspects of data science, but they do not define the field.

The Elements of Data Science

Now that we have defined data science within the context of managing a business, we can start describing the elements of data science. The best way to unpack the art and craft of data science is Drew Conway's often-cited Venn diagram, as shown in *Figure 1.3. (Conway, D. (2010). (The data science Venn diagram—*http://drewconway.com/zia/2013/3/26/the-data-science-venn-diagram*). Downloaded 27 January 2019)*

Conway defines three competencies that a data scientist, or a data science team as a collective, need to possess. The diagram positions data science as an interdisciplinary activity with three dimensions: domain knowledge, mathematics, and computer science. A data scientist is somebody who understands the subject matter under consideration in mathematical terms and writes computer code to solve problems.

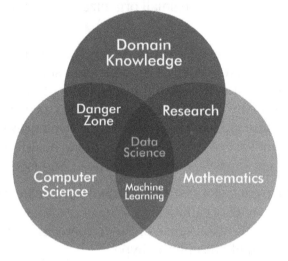

Figure 1.3: Conway's data science Venn diagram

Domain Knowledge

The most significant skill within a data science function is domain knowledge. While the results of advanced applied mathematics such as machine learning are impressive, without understanding the reality that these models describe, they are devoid of meaning and can cause more harm than good. Anyone analyzing a problem needs to understand the context of the issues and the potential solutions. The subject of data science is not the data itself, but the reality this data describes. Data science is about things and people in the real world, not about numbers and algorithms.

A domain expert understands the impact of any confounding variables on the outcomes. An experienced subject-matter expert can quickly perform a sanity check on the process and results of the analysis. Domain knowledge is essential because each area of expertise uses a different paradigm to understand the world.

Each domain of human enquiry or activity has different methodologies to collect and analyze data. Analyzing objective engineering data follows a different approach to subjective data about people or unstructured data in a corpus of text. The analyst needs to be familiar with the tools of the trade within the problem domain. The example of a graduate professional beating a team of machine learning experts with a linear regression shows the importance of domain knowledge.

Domain expertise can also become a source of bias and prevent innovative ways of looking at information. Solutions developed through systematic research can contradict long-held beliefs about a specific topic that are sometimes hard to shift. Implementing data science is thus as much a cultural process as it is a scientific one, which is the topic of *Chapter 4, The Data-Driven Organization.*

Mathematical Knowledge

The analyst uses mathematical skills to convert data into actionable insights. Mathematics consists of pure mathematics as a science, and applied mathematics that helps us to solve problems. The scope of applied mathematics is broad, and data science is opportunistic in choosing the most suitable method. Various types of regression models, graph theory, k-means clustering, decision trees, and so on, are some of the favorite tools of a data scientist. The creative application of complex applied mathematics is one of the two distinguishing factors between traditional business analysis and data science.

Combining subject-matter expertise with mathematical skills is the domain of traditional research and analysis. The notion of conventional research is, however, evolving toward using the principles of data science by using reproducible computer code and sharing the source data through websites such as FigShare (https://figshare.com/).

Numbers are the foundations of mathematics, and the craft of quantitative science is to describe our analogue reality in a model that we can manipulate to predict the future. Not all mathematical skills are necessarily about numbers but can also revolve around logical relationships between words and concepts. Contemporary numerical methods help us to understand relationships between people, the logical structure of a text, and many other aspects beyond the realm of traditional numeric analysis.

Computer Science

Not that long ago, most of the information collected by an organization was stored on paper and archived in copious volumes of arch lever files. Analyzing this information was an arduous task that involved many hours of transcribing information into a format that is useful for analysis.

In the twenty-first century, almost all data is an electronic resource. To create value from this resource, data engineers extract it from a database, combine it with other sources, and clean the data before analysts can make sense of it. This requirement implies that a data scientist needs to have computing skills. Conway uses the term hacking skills, which many people interpret as negative. Conway is, however, not referring to a hacker in the sense of somebody who nefariously uses computers, but in the original meaning of the word as a developer with creative computing skills. The core competency of a hacker, developer, coder, or whatever other term might be preferable, is algorithmic thinking and understanding the logic of data structures. These competencies are vital in extracting and cleaning data to prepare it for the next step of the data science process.

The importance of hacking skills for a data scientist implies that we should move away from point-and-click systems and spreadsheets and instead write code in a suitable programming language. The flexibility and power of a programming language far exceed the capabilities of graphical user interfaces and leads to reproducible analysis, as discussed in *Chapter 2, Good Data Science*.

The mathematical interpretation of reality needs to be translated into computer code. One of the factors that spearheaded data science into popularity is that the available toolkit has grown substantially in the past ten years. Open source computing languages such as R and Python can implement complex algorithms that were previously the domain of specialized software and supercomputers. Open source software has accelerated innovation in how we analyze data and has placed complex machine learning within reach of anyone who is willing to try to learn the skills.

Conway defines the **danger zone** as the area where domain knowledge and computing skills combine, without a good grounding in mathematics. Somebody might have enough computing skills to be pushing buttons on a business intelligence platform or spreadsheet. The user-friendliness of some analysis platforms can be detrimental to the outcomes of the analysis because they create the illusion of accuracy. **Point-and-click** analysis hides the inner workings from the user, creating a black-box result. Although the data might be perfectly structured, valid and reliable, a wrongly applied analytical method leads to useless outcomes.

The Unicorn Data Scientist?

Conway's diagram is often cited in the literature on data science. His simple model helped to define the craft of data science. Other data scientists have proposed more complex models, but they all originate with Conway's basic idea.

The diagram illustrates that the difference between traditional research skills or business analytics lies in the ability to understand and write code. A data scientist understands the problem they seek to resolve, they have the mathematical expertise to analyze the problem, and they possess the computing skills to convert this knowledge into outcomes.

It could be argued that the so-called skills are missing from this picture. However, communication, managing people, facilitating change and so on, are competencies that belong to every professional who works in a complex environment, not just the data scientist.

Some critics of this idea point out that these people are unicorns – that is, they don't exist. Data scientists that possess all these skills are mythical employees that don't exist in the real world. Most data scientists start from either mathematics or computer science, after which it is hard to become a domain expert. This book is written from the point of view that we can breed unicorns by teaching domain experts how to write code and, where required, enhance their mathematical skills.

The Purpose of Data Science

In summary, the promises of data science within organizations have gained a lot of popularity over the past six years. The downside of this popularity is that self-proclaimed futurists have exaggerated the benefits of a strategic and systematic approach to analyzing data. To obtain value from this new approach to using data requires a pragmatic approach beyond the hype. For most organizations, data science will look very differently from the digital utopia portrayed in popular publications.

This chapter defines data science as the strategic and systematic use of data to create value for organizations or society overall. The purpose of using data to improve how organizations perform is to reduce bias in decisions. The original objections that Frederick Taylor held against rules of thumb more than a century ago still stands. Computational analysis of data is a valuable tool to achieve this reduced bias in deciding about future courses of action.

Data science is an interdisciplinary activity that combines domain knowledge with competencies in mathematics and computer science. The data revolution of the past decades has caused an exponential increase in available data, computing capabilities and open source software. Data science is paradoxically not a science about data but a scientific way to use data to influence reality positively. Expertise about the reality under consideration, or domain knowledge, drives data science. Mathematics and computer science are the tools that enable a deeper understanding of our reality and help us to optimize our decisions.

Now that we have an idea of what data science is and what it consists of, we need to define what good data science looks like. The following chapter expands on this description of data science by presenting a normative model of data science. This model defines best practice as the useful, sound and aesthetic analysis of data.

Good Data Science

Introduction

Data is sometimes called the "new oil", a source of new-found wealth that is mined from the depths of corporate and government archives. Some accountants are so excited about the potential value of data that they account for it in the same way as a physical asset. While it is indeed true that data can increase the value of an organization, this resource has no intrinsic value. Just like oil, data needs to be mined and must be refined to the right quality. Data needs to be transported through information networks before it can be used to create new value. The value of data is not in the information itself but occurs during the transformations it undergoes.

The analogy between data and oil is only partially correct in that data is an infinite resource. The same data can be used many times for a sometimes originally unintended purpose. The ability to use data for more than one goal is one of the reasons data science has gained popularity around board tables. Senior managers are seeking ways to extract value from so-called 'dark data'. Data scientists use these forgotten data sources to create new knowledge, make better decisions, and spawn innovations.

The question that arises from this introduction is how to manage and analyze data so it can become a valuable resource. This chapter presents a normative model to create value from data using three basic principles derived from architecture. This model is useful for data scientists as an internal check to ensure that their activities maximize value. Managers can use this model to assess the outcomes of a data science project without having to understand the mathematical intricacies of the craft and science of analysis.

A Data Science Trivium

Although data science is a quintessentially twenty-first-century activity, to define good data science, we can find inspiration from a Roman architect and engineer who lived two thousand years ago. Vitruvius is immortalized through his book *About Architecture*, which inspired Leonardo Da Vinci to draw his famous Vitruvian man. Vitruvius wrote that an ideal building must exhibit three qualities: **utilitas**, **firmitas**, and **venustas**, or usefulness, soundness, and aesthetics.

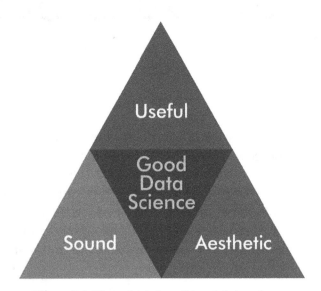

Figure 2.1: The principles of good data science

Buildings must have utility so they can be used for their intended purpose. A house needs to be functional and comfortable; a theatre needs to be designed so that everybody can see the stage. Each type of building has its functional requirements. Secondly, buildings must be sound in that they are firm enough to withstand the forces that act upon them. Finally, buildings need to be aesthetic. In the words of Vitruvius, buildings need to look like Venus, the Roman goddess of beauty and seduction.

The Vitruvian rules for architecture can also be applied to the products of data science. (*Lankow, J., Ritchie, J., & Crooks, R. (2012). Infographics: The Power of Visual Storytelling. Hoboken, N.J: John Wiley & Sons, Inc*) Great data science needs to have utility; it needs to be useful to create value. The analysis should be sound so it can be trusted. The products of data science also need to be aesthetic, as in, easily understood, in order to maximize the value, they provide to an organization, as shown in *Figure 2.1*.

Useful Data Science

How do we know that something is useful? The simple, but not very illuminating answer is that when something is useful, it has utility. Some philosophers interpret utility as the ability to provide the greatest good for the highest number of people. This definition is quite compelling, but it requires contextualization. What is right in one situation might not be so beneficial in another.

The concept of the highest number of people is also open to interpretation. Is something only useful when it benefits all of humanity, or can it also be useful when it helps just one person? The requirement to include the highest number of people in our definition of usefulness might work well for government organizations. It is also not so clear in corporations that seek to maximize the benefits to their shareholders.

Whether something is useful or useless depends on the context in which it is applied, but also on the set of values by which it is judged. Defining usefulness in generic terms will prove to be an impossible quest because of the dependence on the context and the relevant value system. For example, for Greenpeace, analyzing data from fracking activities will have a different usefulness that it would for a gas exploration company. The same data can satisfy different types of merit depending on context.

These philosophical deliberations aside, defining usefulness for organizations is more straightforward because we apply a pragmatic approach. Usefulness in terms of organizations is the extent to which something contributes to their strategic or operational objectives. If the result of a data science project is unable to meet this criterion, then it is, strictly speaking, useless. As a civil engineer and social scientist, I could spend many hours analyzing the vast amounts of data collected by my organization. Dredging the data to find something of value might be an exciting way to waste time; there is also a significant risk of finding fool's gold instead of valuable nuggets of wisdom. The first step that anyone working with data should undertake before starting a project is to define the business problem that needs solving.

This book follows a pragmatic and perspectivist view of usefulness. For a data science strategy to be successful, it must facilitate the objectives of the organization. Data scientists are opportunistic in the approach they use to resolve problems. Perspectivism implies that the same data can be used for different issues, depending on the perspective you take on the available information and the problem at hand.

After digesting a research report or viewing a visualization, managers should ask themselves: "What do I do differently today as a result?" Usefulness in data science depends on the ability of the results to empower professionals to influence reality positively. In other words, the result of data science should either comfort management that objectives have been met or provide actionable insights to resolve existing problems or prevent future ones.

Providing actionable intelligence is only a narrow scope of the work of a data scientist. The concept of usefulness in business needs to be extended beyond this short term and one-dimensional view. Business scholar Bernard Jaworski classified the results of research into two types to help us make sense of how theory relates to practice (*Jaworski, B.J. (2011). On managerial relevance. Journal of Marketing, 75(4), 211–224. (doi 10.1509/jmkg.75.4.211*–https://doi.org/10.1509/jmkg.75.4.211). Some knowledge is suitable for action, which is the much sought-after actionable intelligence. Other research doesn't lead to action but inspires deeper thinking about managerial practice. Data science can direct action, but it can also motivate innovation by providing a more profound understanding of the current reality. The results of data science should either stimulate action or inspire contemplation. While the relevance of acting is self-evident, reflection is not often recognized as a beneficial managerial impact.

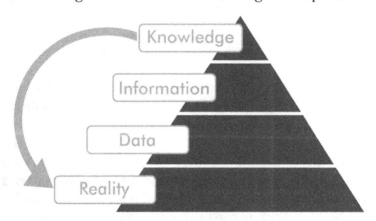

Figure 2.2: The Reality, Data, Information, Knowledge Pyramid

For data science to provide actionable intelligence, the raw data needs to be converted to knowledge following a standardized workflow. The well-known **DIKW Pyramid** (Data, Information, Knowledge, and Wisdom) explains how data produces a useful analysis. The source of the original version of this model is lost in time, as a multitude of authors has used it without citation. The basic principle of the hierarchy is that to obtain wisdom, you need to have relevant knowledge, which derives from information, which in turn consists of the conclusions drawn from the data. Various versions of the model have been proposed, with slightly different terminology and interpretations.

The version of the Pyramid in this book is modified to better understand how to create useful data science, as shown in *Figure* 2.2. Firstly, wisdom no longer forms part of the model, because this concept is too nebulous to be useful. Anyone seeking wisdom should study philosophy or practice religion, as data science is unable to provide this need. Secondly, the bottom of the pyramid needs to be grounded. The standard DIKW model ignores the reality from which the data is collected that creates the information and knowledge used to make business decisions. The second addition to the traditional model is a feedback loop from knowledge to the real world. The purpose of data science is to enhance the knowledge that professionals use to influence reality by converting data into information.

Reality

Useful data science positively influences reality by collecting data, creating information, and increasing our knowledge about and understanding of reality. This knowledge is useful when it changes the way we perceive reality to innovate the way we do things, and when it enables better operational or strategic decisions. If data science becomes abstracted from the world it seeks to understand or influence, it loses its power to be valuable.

This reality of data science can be either physical or social, each of which requires a different paradigm to describe the world. Our physical reality can be measured with almost arbitrary precision. We can measure size, weight, chemical composition, time and so on, with high validity and reliability.

The social world can also be summarized in numbers, but these measurements are almost always indirect. We cannot read people's minds. When we want to know how somebody feels about a level of service or another psychological parameter, we can only indirectly measure this variable. Data from the social world is often qualitative and requires different considerations than in the physical world.

The complex relationship between the data and the reality it seeks to improve emphasizes the need for subject-matter expertise about the problem under consideration. Data should never be merely an abstract series of numbers or a corpus of text and images but should always be interpreted in its context to do justice to the reality it describes.

Data

Data is the main ingredient of data science, but not all data sources provide the same opportunities to create useful data products. The quality and quantity of the data determine its value to the organization. This mechanism is just another way of stating the classic **Garbage-In-Garbage-Out** (**GIGO**) principle. This principle derives from the fact that computers blindly follow instructions, irrespective of truthfulness, usefulness, or ethical consequences of the outcomes. An amazing algorithm with low quality or insufficient data will be unable to deliver value to an organization. On the other hand, great data with an invalid algorithm will also result in garbage, instead of valuable information.

The quality of data relates to the measurement processes used to collect the information and the relationship of this process to the reality it describes. The quality of the data and the outcome of the analysis is expressed in their validity and reliability. The *Sound Data Science* section discusses the soundness of data and information in more detail.

The next step is to decide how much data to collect. Determining the appropriate amount of data is a balancing act between the cost of collecting, storing, and analyzing the data versus the potential usefulness of the outcome. In some instances, collecting the required data can be more costly than the benefits it provides.

The recent steep reduction in the cost of collecting and storing data seems to render the need to be selective in data gathering a moot point. Data scientists might claim that we should collect everything, because a time machine is much more expensive than collecting and storing more data than strictly necessary. Not measuring parts of a process has an opportunity cost because future benefits might not be realized. This opportunity cost needs to be balanced with the estimated cost of collecting and storing data.

This revolution in data gathering is mainly related to physical measurements and the so-called Internet of Things, mobile phones, and other wearable devices. Measurement devices and the transmission and storage of data are more affordable, so carpet-bombing a region with sensors to collect data becomes more feasible. Some aspects of reality remain complicated and expensive to measure, as the Internet of Things cannot be applied everywhere. Assessing how people feel about something, their intentions, and so on will, until we have access to cost-effective mass mind reading, remain a complicated and expensive undertaking.

One guideline to determine what and how often to collect is to work backward from the sought benefits. Following the knowledge pyramid, we should collect data that enables us to influence reality positively. The frequency of collection is an outcome of the statistical power that is required to achieve the desired objectives. In most cases, the more data available, the higher the statistical power of the analysis.

The amount of data points required to achieve a specific outcome also depends on the type of data. The more reliable and valid the measurements, the fewer the data points needed to obtain a reliable sample. Lastly, the need to ensure that a sample represents the population it describes defines the minimal size of the sample in a social context. Determining sample sizes is a complex topic and the statistics literature provides detailed information about how much data to collect to achieve the required statistical power.

Gathering data about people because it might be useful in the future also has ethical consequences. Storing large amounts of personal data without a defined need can be considered unethical because the data might be used for a purpose for which the subjects did not consent. Medical records are a case in point. They are collected to manage our health and not for insurance companies to maximize their profits. The *Ethical Data Science* section of this book discusses the ethics of data science.

The following case study illustrates how to decide the ideal amount of data to collect. A water utility discussed how much data they wanted to gather to measure how much water customers use. The existing method only provided one data point for each water meter every three months. The water engineers would ideally have liked a reading every five minutes, while the billing department was more than happy with one daily reading.

New technology became available that collects data at a higher frequency. However, the higher the rate, the higher the cost of collection due to transmission bandwidth and battery life. Collecting data every five minutes was unfeasible and potentially unethical because it reveals too much about the lifestyles of customers. Daily data was insufficient to provide benefits in network design and operation. The utility decided to collect hourly data because it allows for most of the sought benefits, doesn't significantly impact the privacy of customers, and is within reasonable reach for the current level of technology.

Information

Within the context of this book, information is defined as processed data. Information is data placed with in context of the reality from which it was extracted. To ensure information is sound and useful, professionals need to use an appropriate methodology, logically present the information, and preserve the results for future reuse or review.

Data scientists use an extensive range of methods to convert data into information. At the lowest level, summarizing the averages of the various data points converts provides some value. More complex analysis transforms data about the past into a prediction of the future. These techniques require a solid understanding of mathematics and analytical methods to ensure they don't result in data pseudo data science.

Communicating information is where art meets data science. Writing good reports and designing meaningful visualizations ensures that a data product is useful.

Lastly, the information needs to be preserved so that it is accessible to those who need it in the future or for those who seek to review the methods.

The last two sections in this chapter discuss the criteria for the soundness of data products and how to best visualize information. *Chapter 3, Strategic Data Science,* delves into the various methods to convert data into information. *Chapter 4, The Data-Driven Organization,* covers some issues concerning communicating the results of data science to other professionals.

Knowledge

Professionals with subject-matter expertise gain knowledge from the results of data science, which they use to decide on future courses of action. Knowledge can be either tacit or explicit. The results of a data science project, or a data product, are explicit knowledge. This knowledge can be transferred through writing or instruction.

Numbers and visualizations help professionals to understand the reality they need to manage. This process of understanding and using these results in practice leads to tacit knowledge, which is the essence of domain expertise. Tacit knowledge is difficult to transfer because it consists of a combination of learned explicit knowledge mediated through practical experience.

Data science thus not only requires domain expertise to be useful, but it can also increase this expertise. This topic is outside the scope of data science as it ventures into knowledge management.

The Feedback Loop

The last and most important part of this data science model is the feedback loop from knowledge back to reality. The arrow signifies actionable intelligence, which is how reality is improved through knowledge. The key message of this section is that the results of data science need to either lead to a different way of thinking about a problem or provide actionable intelligence.

Either option eventually leads to improved decisions using the best available data and analysis. Care needs to be taken, however, that the correct conclusions are drawn. The GIGO principle only covers the input of the process, but the process itself also needs to be sound. Although the data might be of good quality, a lousy analysis will still result in garbage. The next two sections discuss how we can ascertain whether the outcomes of a given application of data science are sound and ensure the user draws the correct conclusion from the information.

Sound Data Science

Just like a building should be sound and not collapse, a data product needs to be sound to be able to create business value. Soundness is where the science and the data meet. The soundness of a data product is defined by the validity and reliability of the analysis, which are well-established scientific principles as shown in *Figure 2.3*. (*Anderson, C. (2015). Creating a Data-Driven Organization: Practical Advice from the Trenches. Sebastopol, CA: O'Reilly Media Inc*) Soundness of data science also requires that the results are reproducible. Lastly, data, and the process of creating data products, need to be governed to assure beneficial outcomes.

The distinguishing difference between traditional forms of business analysis and data science is the systematic approach to solving problems. The key word in the term *data science* is thus not *data*, but *science*. Data science is only useful when the data answers a useful question, which is the science part of the process. (*Caffo, B., Peng, R., & Leek, J.T. (2018). Executive Data Science. A Guide to Training and Managing the Best Data Scientists. LeanPub*)

This systematic approach ensures that the outcomes of data science can be relied upon to decide on alternative courses of action. Systematic data science uses the principles of scientific enquiry, but it is more pragmatic in its approach. While scientists search for general truths to explain the world, data scientists pragmatically seek to solve problems. The basic principles that underpin this methodical approach are the validity, reliability, and reproducibility of the data, the methods, and the results.

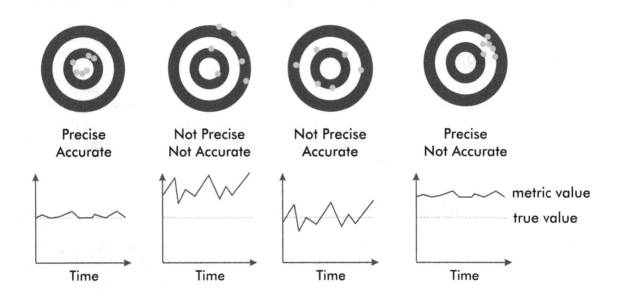

Figure 2.3: Visualizing validity and reliability

Validity

The validity of a dataset and the information derived from it relates to the extent to which the data matches the reality it describes. The validity of data and information depends on how this information was collected and how it was analyzed.

For physical measurements, validity relates to the technology used to measure the world and is determined by physics or chemistry. If, for example, our variable of interest is temperature, we use the fact that materials expand, or their electrical resistance increases, when the temperature rises. Measuring length relies on comparing it with a calibrated unit or the time it takes light to travel in a vacuum. Each type of physical measurement uses a physical or chemical process, and the laws of nature define validity. When measuring pH, for example, we want to be sure that we measure the power of hydrogen ions, and not some other chemical property.

Psychological processes, such as customer satisfaction or personality, are much harder to measure than physical properties. Although a state of mind is merely a pattern of electrical and chemical activity in the brain, no technology can directly measure it. Not much is known about the relationship between the physical events in the brain and our feelings, motivations, and other psychological states.

Not all data about people has a validity problem. Observations that relate directly to our behaviors, such as technology that tracks our movements, or eye-tracking equipment to record our gaze, are physical measurements. Demographic data is a direct measurement of a social state. However, even seemingly simple aspects such as gender can lead to significant complexity when trying to measure it. What often seems a simple demographic variable can be quite complicated to define.

Scientists use complex machinery to scan brains to discover how our mind functions. Marketers regularly use this technology to understand customers. Neuromarketing produces insights from brain scans to fine-tune the design of products and marketing communication to maximize the likelihood that a customer purchases their offering. (*Lindström, M. (2010). Buyology: Truth and Lies About Why We Buy. New York: Broadway Books*) Brain scanning gives insight into the processes inside our brain, but it is quite expensive and intrusive. Scanning technologies are insightful, but not an efficient way to get to know your customers.

In practice, social scientists and psychologists use psychometrics to indirectly measure states of mind by using survey techniques. We might ask a customer whether they agree or disagree with a series of statements, such as "The hotel room was comfortable". Most commonly, these questions are measured using a Likert scale with five or seven descriptors.

The basic principle of surveys to measure a state of mind is that the mental processes we seek to understand cause the subject to answer a survey question in a certain way. People who think that the hotel room was very comfortable will fully agree with the statement in the survey. The statistical analysis of such questions seeks to reverse this causality to learn about the subject's thoughts and feelings.

The variables that we are interested in are latent variables, because they are hidden within the mind of the subject and only reveal themselves indirectly through the survey answers. The validity of psychometric measurements is a complex topic with many types of validity, each with their specific purpose. A vast field of literature describes how to measure and analyze latent variables. (*DeVellis, R.F. (2011). Scale Development: Theory and Applications (3rd ed.). SAGE Publications*)

Another method to understand people is to use a big data approach. This technology does not rely on surveys or brain scans from a sample of the population but uses our behavior on social media or measured through a wearable device as a proxy for our psychology. The big data approach is entirely different from any of the other techniques.

Brain scanning and psychometrics aim to understand future behavior by indirectly measuring what we think, feel and believe. One of the main problems with surveys is that our answers are biased and perhaps not an accurate reflection of what we believe. Brain scans are impressive but are still only a proxy for our internal states of mind.

Big data methods measure our actual behavior by recording what we purchase, where we travel, what we search for and so on. The second significant difference between big data and traditional approaches is that the first two methods rely on a small sample of the population, while big data approaches, by their very nature, include millions of subjects. The validity of this information is very high because it measures actual behavior instead of indirect parameters.

Reliability

The reliability or accuracy of physical measurements depends on the quality of the instrumentation used to obtain the data. Engineers spend a lot of effort to assure the reliability of instrumentation through maintenance and calibration programs. The instruments need to be installed and maintained to the manufacturer's specifications to ensure their ongoing accuracy. Quality assurance of instrumentation is possibly the costliest aspect of collecting and storing data about physical processes.

Several methods exist to test the reliability of psychological survey data. One simple test is to check for respondents that provide the same answer to all questions. The chances that somebody would genuinely answer "Neither agree or disagree" to all questions is negligible, and it is good practice to remove these people from the sample. Researchers also use questions to trap fake responses. The researcher can, for example, ask people whether they agree or disagree with certain factual statements, such as: "You live in Australia." Any subject not wholly agreeing with this question (assuming this is an Australian survey) should be removed from the sample.

Brain scanning technology relies on small samples of the population because of the cost of the technology. These methods are sensitive to error, illustrated by an infamous example. Craig Bennett and Abigail Baird placed a dead Atlantic salmon in an fMRI scanner and were surprised to find brain activity. They published their results to warn scientists of the risk of unreliable statistical methods. The spoof scientific journal *Annals of Improbable Research* awarded Bennet and Baird with the Ig Nobel prize. This annual prize awards unusual and trivial results in science. (*Bennett, C.M., Baird, A.A., Miller, M.B., & Wolford, G.L. (2009). Neural correlates of interspecies perspective taking in the post-mortem Atlantic Salmon: an argument for multiple comparisons correction. NeuroImage, 47, S1251*–https://doi.org/10.1016/S1053-8119(09)71202-9).

The reliability of big data approaches is arguably very high because people provide this information not to satisfy the need of a researcher but to guide their actions. Rather than asking somebody whether they will purchase something in the future, our actual purchase patterns are naturally a strong predictor for future purchases.

Reproducibility

The third aspect of the soundness of a data product is its **reproducibility**, which is the ability for other people to reconstruct the workflow of the analyst from raw data collection to reporting. This requirement is a distinguishing factor between traditional business analysis and data science. The condition of reproducibility ensures that managers who base business decisions on a data product can review how the results were obtained, or at least have trust in the results because they are potentially auditable. Reproducibility ensures that peers can evaluate all analysis and negates the problems of black boxes.

Replication is the gold standard for science to ensure the quality of previous results. Replication involves repeating the experiments, which is a costly and complex activity. The past few years, some areas of science have suffered from a replication crisis. Famous experiments in psychology and sociology are under a cloud of doubt because current researchers fail to replicate the findings. Some scientists were clearly fraudulent in their approach, changing data and manipulating the analytical process to obtain the desired results. Other scientists either used unrepresentative samples or misinterpreted the data and published wrong results. The peer review process did not identify these issues because the authors only provided the outcomes of their research, and the papers were published and accepted as truthful.

This crisis in some of the sciences has moved some journals to require authors to submit not only the written text but also the data and analytical code that was used to draw the conclusions. Releasing the data and the code strengthens peer review. These principles of reproducibility also apply to business analysis and ensure sound data science. Every study needs to be undertaken in such a way that a colleague or auditor can recreate the steps of the recipe that was followed to reach a conclusion.

The most effective method to achieve full reproducibility is to use literate programming. This method combines computer code with text so that the analysis becomes fully transparent. Although many systems exist that at first instance might seem more user-friendly than writing code, point-and-click systems have severe limitations, and the results are often difficult to verify. *Chapter 4, The Data-Driven Organization,* discusses the various tools to create data products in more detail.

A specific aspect of machine learning that relates to its reproducibility is whether the user can understand how the model drew a conclusion. Can the data scientist explain to the subject-matter expert how the model works? The great benefit of machine learning is that these algorithms can detect patterns in large volumes of data that are impossible for humans to comprehend within a lifetime. Often, however, machine learning results in a black box that converts data into output. Although the algorithms are reproducible in that they produce the same result with the same data, they are not necessarily explainable. The outcomes of, for example, a random forest model, can take tens of pages to print and the logic will be hard to verify for humans.

Machine learning algorithms are sometimes simplified so that the responsible managers can understand the logic of the decisions they make. In these cases, reliability is sacrificed for greater explainability. Whether a data science product is explainable depends not only on the code itself but also on the level of mathematical insight of the consumer of the outcomes. Explainability is thus a direct result of the level of data literacy of the organization. This theme is further discussed in *Chapter 4, The Data-Driven Organization.*

Governance

The fourth aspect of sound data science is governance. The process of creating data products needs to be documented in line with quality assurance principles. Practical considerations such as naming conventions for scripts, coding standards to ensure readability and so on are a necessary evil when managing complex data science projects.

The same principle also applies to managing data. Each data source in an organization needs to have an owner and a custodian who understands the relationship between this data and the reality from which it is extracted. Large organizations have formal processes that ensure each dataset is governed and that all employees use a single source of truth to safeguard the soundness of data products.

Governance is a double-edged sword, as it can become the 'wet blanket' of an organization. When governance becomes too strict, it will smother the very innovation that data science is expected to deliver. The art of managing a data science team is to find a middle way between strictly following the process and allowing for deviations of the norm to foster innovation. Good governance minimizes risk, while at the same time enabling positive deviance that leads to better outcomes.

Aesthetic Data Science

Vitruvius insisted that buildings, or any other structure, should be beautiful. The aesthetics of a building causes more than just a pleasant feeling. Architecturally designed places stimulate our thinking, increase our well-being, improve our productivity and stimulate creativity.

While it is evident that buildings need to be pleasing to the eye, the aesthetics of data products might not be so obvious. The requirement for aesthetic data science is not a call for beautification and obfuscation of the ugly details of the results. The process of cleaning and analyzing data is inherently complex. Presenting the results of this process is a form of storytelling that reduces this complexity to ensure that a data product is understandable.

The data science value chain starts with reality, described by data. This data is converted to knowledge, which managers use to influence reality to meet their objectives. This chain from reality to human knowledge contains four transformations, each with opportunities for a loss of validity and reliability. The last step in the value chain requires the user of the results of data science to interpret the information to draw the correct conclusion about their future course of action. Reproducibility is one of the tools to minimize the chance of misinterpretation of analyses. Another mechanism to ensure proper interpretation is to produce aesthetic data science.

Aesthetic data science is about creating a data product, which can be a visualization or a report, that is designed so that the user draws correct conclusions. A messy graph or an incomprehensible report limits the value that can be extracted from the information. The remainder of this section provides some guidelines on designing good visualizations and writing reports.

Visualization

Data visualizations are everywhere. They are no longer the domain of scientific publications and business reports. Publications in every medium use graph to tell stories. The internet is awash with infographics on a wide range of topics. These popular images are often data science visuals because they are designed to entertain, with limited usability from a business perspective. They are a fantastic tool to supply information to customers but should not be used to report data science.

Aesthetics and usefulness go hand in hand. Some data visualizations in engineering remind me of a Jackson Pollock painting, with a multitude of lines and colors splashed over the screen. Adding too much information to a graph and using too many colors reduces its usability. When visualization is not aesthetic, it becomes harder to interpret which leads to the wrong conclusions and can even deceive the user. (Jones, G. E. (2007). How to Lie with Charts (2nd ed). Santa Monica, Calif: LaPuerta)

Chapter 1, What is Data Science? discussed how Taylor introduced the concept of scientific management to remove bias from business decisions. A data scientist needs to be aware of these biases in order to prevent them and create data products that don't deceive. Many of these biases relate to how information is presented.

Our perception is not always an accurate representation of reality, and we often misinterpret the images that our retina collects. Optical illusions are funny internet memes, but they also occur in real life. Besides optical illusions, messy visualizations are hard to interpret because our mind does not know which element to focus on. A messy graphic confuses the brain so that it starts to form its interpretations.

Perhaps a good data visualization should look more like a painting by Piet Mondrian, who is famous for his austere compositions with straight lines and primary colors. Using art to explain data visualization is not an accidental metaphor because visual art represents how the artist perceives reality. This comparison between Pollock and Mondrian is not a judgement of their artistic abilities. For Pollock, reality was chaotic and messy, while Mondrian saw a geometric order behind the perceived world.

Although visualizing data has some parallels with art, it is very different. All art is basically a form of deception. The artist paints a three-dimensional image on a flat canvas, and although we see people, we are just looking at blobs of paint. Data visualization as an art form needs to be truthful and not deceive, either intentionally or accidentally. The purpose of any visualization is to validly and reliably reflect reality.

Aesthetic data science is not so much an art as it is a craft. Following some basic rules will prevent confusing the consumers of data products. Firstly, a visualization needs to have a straightforward narrative. Secondly, visualizing data should be as simple as possible, minimizing elements that don't add to the story.

- **Storytelling:** First and foremost, a visualization needs to tell a story. The story in data visualization should not be a mystery novel or of the choose your own adventure genre. A visualization should not have suspense but get straight to the point. Trying to squeeze too much information into one graph will confuse the reader. Ideally, each visualization should contain only one or two narratives. If there is more to tell, then use more charts and create a dashboard.

Numerical data can contain several types of narratives. A graph can compare data points to show a trend among items or communicate differences between them. Bar charts are the best option to compare data points with each other. A line graph is possibly your best option to compare data points over time. The distribution of data points is best visualized using a histogram. Scatter plots or bubble charts show relationships between two or three variables, as shown in *Figure 2.4*.

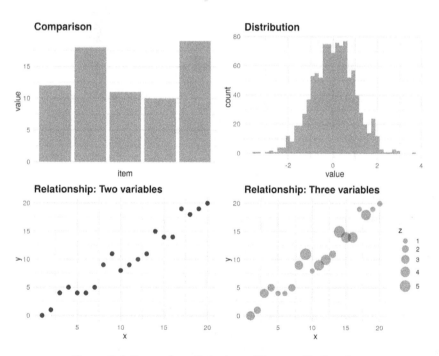

Figure 2.4: Examples of stories with quantitative data

The detailed considerations of choosing the most suitable visualization are outside the scope of this book. The Chart Chooser website, https://chartchooser.com, provides a dynamic interface to choose the best graph to tell a story. The main point is that every visualization needs to tell a story, and not just summarize a bunch of data.

Visualizing qualitative information has its own language, with many options for telling a story. Displaying qualitative information is more of an art than a craft because there is less reliance on mathematics. Word clouds are a popular tool to summarize text. These visualizations display the relative frequency of the words in a text, as shown in *Figure* 2.5. Network diagrams are another common visualization tool. Networks are a convenient method to analyze relationships between people or other qualitative entities, such as journal articles.

Figure 2.5: A word cloud of a draft version of this chapter with the top 25 words.

- **Visualization Design:** Beauty is in the eye of the beholder, and there are no formulas or algorithms to ensure perfect visualizations. The social network Reddit has two groups dedicated to visualizations. Users members of the (Data is Ugly (https://reddit.com/r/dataisugly/) and Data is Beautiful (https://reddit.com/r/dataisbeautiful/)) groups share images of visualizations they consider ugly or beautiful. These two groups sometimes share the same visualizations because of different interpretations of aesthetics in data. What is a beautiful visualization to one person, is an abomination to somebody else? The aesthetics of data visualization is, for the most part, in the eye of the beholder. However, when viewing aesthetics from a practical perspective, we can define what this means with a simple heuristic.

Edward Tufte is an American statistician who is famous for his work on visualization. (*Tufte, E. R. (1997). Visual Explanations: Images and Quantities, Evidence and Narrative. Cheshire, Conn.: Graphics Press*) Tufte introduced the concept of the data-ink ratio. In simple terms, this ratio expresses the relationship between the ink on the paper that tells a story and the total amount of ink on the paper. Tufte argues that this ratio should be as close to one as possible. In other words, we should not use any graphical elements that don't communicate any information, such as background images, superfluous lines and text.

Now that we are in the paperless era, we can use the data-pixel ratio as a generic measure for the aesthetics of visualizations. The principle is the same as in the analogue days. Remove any redundant information in your visualization. Unnecessary lines, multiple colors, or multiple narratives risk confusing the user of the report.

The **data-ink ratio** is not a mathematical concept that needs to be expressed in exact numbers. This ratio is a guideline for designers of visualizations to help them decide what to include and, more importantly, what to exclude from an image.

Figure 2.6 shows an example of maximizing the data-ink ratio. The bar chart on the left has a meagre **data-pixel** ratio. The background image of a cat might be cute and possibly even related to the topic of the visualization, but it only distracts from the message. Using colors to identify the variables is unnecessary because the labels are at the bottom of the graph. The legend is not very functional because it also duplicates the labels. Lastly, the lines around the bars have no function.

To improve this version, all unnecessary graphical elements have been removed. If the story of this graph is to compare variables, the columns have been ranked from large too small. If the narrative of this graph was to compare one or more of the variables with other variables, then groups of bars can be colored to indicate the categories.

The basic rule of visually communicating data is to not 'pimp' your visualizations with unnecessary graphical elements or text that does not add to the story. When visualizing data, austerity is best practice.

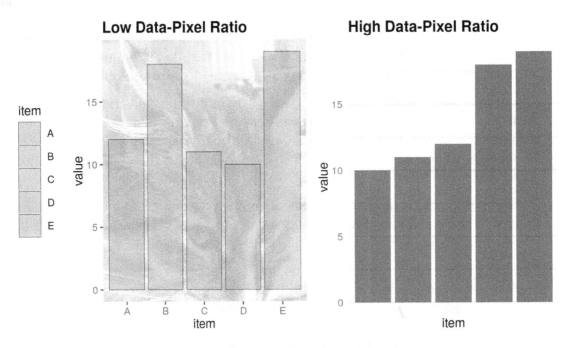

Figure 2.6: Examples of the data-pixel ratio

- **A Splash of Color:** In the era before the petrochemical revolution, colors were mostly limited to nature because artificial coloring was very expensive. The purple togas of Roman emperors were dyed with the secretions of thousands of sea snails. Seventeenth-century Dutch painter Johannes Vermeer used precious lapis lazuli to obtain the perfect blue for his paintings. The expense of creating colors in the past limited the art of choosing the right ones to artists and rich people.

  In our times, we have easy access to every imaginable color. We can buy clothes in whatever color or desire or paint our house like Pippi Longstocking's villa. We are spoilt for choice concerning color. The increased possibilities are also a burden because we need to choose the right color, not just any color. This tyranny of choice also plays a role in designing beautiful visualizations.

When buying clothing or painting a house, our choice of colors is hopefully governed by a sense of style. When designing visualizations, color plays a more instrumental role. The colors in a graph are not decoration, but they communicate a narrative. The basic principle for good visualization design is to minimize the number of colors.

Colors have intrinsic meaning that helps to tell the story. Red is generally recognized as a warning sign and green a calmer tone. In Western cultures, pink is associated with femininity and blue is often used in a corporate sense. Marketers use these associations with color when designing brands. The psychological meaning of color is, however, not culturally constant and can vary between countries. The Color Psychology website, https://www.colorpsychology.org, contains valuable information about how colors are interpreted.

Traffic lights are one of the most popular color schemes in business reporting. Red stands for an adverse outcome, yellow for a neutral one and green is positive. This type of reporting helps managers to focus on problem areas so they can discuss actions to improve future performance. A note of caution is that this technique does not work for men with green/red color blindness. This condition is not a problem with real traffic lights, as the order of the lights is always the same. However, on a business report, the colors will all look the same to roughly eight per cent of men with this condition.

The minimum amount of color depends on the narrative you want to convey and the type of visualization. **Cartography** often uses color to communicate its message. One of the problems that plagued mathematicians for centuries is how many colors we need as a minimum to color every area on a map, without two bordering regions having the same color. Cartographers know from practical experience that this number is four, but mathematical proof only came in a few decades ago.

Besides minimizing the number of colors, we also need to know which colors to use. Cartographers Mark Harrower and Cynthia Brewer developed the Color Brewer system, at http://colorbrewer2.org/, to help designers of visualizations select a good scheme. These color schemes are designed for **choropleth maps** but can also be used for non-spatial visualizations. (*Harrower, M., & Brewer, C.A. (2003). ColorBrewer.org: An Online Tool for Selecting Color Schemes for Maps. The Cartographic Journal, 40(1), 27–371*–https://doi.org/10.1179/000870403235002042) The Color Brewer system consists of three types of color palates: sequential, diverging, and qualitative, as shown in *Figure* 2.7.

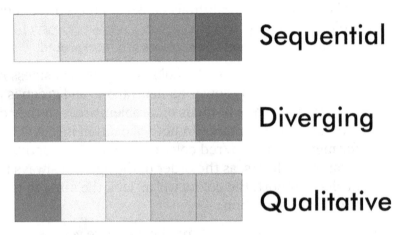

Figure 2.7: Types of color schemes.

Sequential schemes contain a series of colors with increasing strength. These color schemes are most suitable to visualize magnitude from low to high, with light colors usually used for low data values and dark colors for high values.

Diverging colors are used to visualize a deviation from a norm, such as droughts or floods, or adherence to a budget. Green, yellow, and red are the most common use of this type of palate, and business reports are filled with traffic lights to report progress.

Qualitative colors are groups of colors that are aesthetically compatible but without a logical relationship between them based on the data. These palates can express qualitative values such as categories. The left graph in *Figure* 2.6 is an example of a qualitative scheme used to indicate categorical variables.

Reports

Advertising executive Fred Barnard coined the now-famous idiom that "a picture is worth (ten) thousand words" in 1927. While this might be the case, the complexity of data science in most cases requires text to explain the analysis.

To claim that a report needs to be written with clarity and precision in proper spelling and grammar almost seems redundant. The importance of readable reports implies that the essential language a data scientist needs to master is not Python or R, but English, or another relevant human language.

Writing a good data report enhances the reproducibility of the process by describing all the steps in the process. A report should also help to explain any complex analysis to the user to engender trust in the results.

The topic of writing good business reports is too broad to do justice within the narrow scope of this book. For those people that need help with their writing, data science can also assist. There are many great online writing tools to support authors not only with spelling but also grammar and idiom. These advanced spelling and grammar checkers use advanced text analysis tools to detect more than spelling mistakes and can help fine-tune a text using data science. As English is my second language, I rely heavily on the Grammarly software to ensure it is free of apparent issues. However, even grammar-checking with machine learning is not a perfect replacement for a human being who understands the meaning of the text.

Best-Practice Data Science

This chapter discusses a normative framework for creating value with data. Inspired by the Roman architect Vitruvius, the products of data science need to be useful, sound and aesthetic.

Data science is useful when the data is converted into information. This information increases the knowledge of the professionals who use it. This knowledge improves the reality from which the data was extracted. The relationship between reality and data is critical.

Data science is sound when it delivers valid and reliable results and can be reviewed by other experts.

Validity is the extent to which the data describes the aspect of reality it is presumed to represent. In physical measurements, this aspect is governed by physics and chemistry. In measures of the social world, validity is complicated, because we can only record the external states of a human being, and not their state of mind.

The reliability of data and its analysis relates to the accuracy of the information. In physical measurements, accuracy is a function of how well an instrument is installed and maintained. Within the social sciences, reliability relates closely to the biases of people providing data.

Sound data science also needs to be reproducible and well governed. Reproducibility is essential to enable other people to understand the steps taken to achieve a result. Governance is a crucial aspect of managing a business and helps to make data science efficient and effective.

Lastly, the results of data science need to be aesthetic to reduce the likelihood that users draw the wrong conclusions. This need for aesthetics does not imply beautification, but rather a focus on telling a story with the data. The basic principle of good visualizations is to minimize text and graphics that does not communicate any information.

The next chapter delves into the strategic aspects of data science by presenting a five-phase framework that organizations can follow to enhance the value they extract from data.

3

Strategic Data Science

Introduction

Managers often claim to be "data-rich but information-poor". This statement is in many cases only partially correct because it hides a misconception about the life cycle of data. Being replete with data but poor concerning information suggests that previously untapped data sources are waiting to be mined and used.

It is highly unlikely that any organization collects data for no particular purpose. Data is in most cases collected to manage operational processes. Collecting data without purpose is a waste of resources. After the data is used, it is stored and becomes 'dark data'. Because almost all business processes are recorded electronically, data is now everywhere. Managers rightly ask themselves what to do with this information after it is archived. A strategic approach to data science helps an organization to unlock the unrealized value of these stores of data to better understand their strategic and operational context.

Whereas the framework in *Chapter 2, Good Data Science*, is normative and defines ideal data science, the model in this chapter describes the path that an organization can take to increase the value they extract from data. The data science continuum is a hierarchical five-phase framework toward becoming a data-driven organization. This chapter discusses the phases of this continuum as a strategy map for data science.

The Data Science Continuum

Strategic data science follows a process where an organization builds competencies toward high-value analysis. The evolution of becoming a data-driven organization starts with collecting data generated during operational processes. The next step involves describing this data using exploratory techniques such as basic visualizations and summary statistics, which is the domain of traditional business reporting.

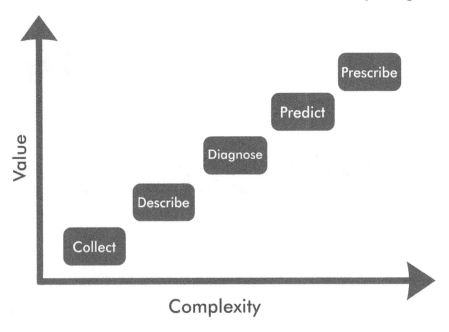

Figure 3.1: The data science continuum

After the data is explored and understood, organizations can diagnose business processes to understand causal and logical relationships between variables. The penultimate phase in the continuum is to use knowledge of the past and its causal and logical connections to predict possible futures and construct the desired future. The final stage in the data science journey is a situation where data is used to prescribe day-to-day operations (*Figure 3.1*).

The continuum is not a journey from left to right, eventually landing at a place where algorithms control our destiny, and the remainder of the continuum becomes less critical. The continuum guides data science strategy toward this point but forms a strict hierarchy. Before algorithms can independently decide anything, you need to be able to predict the immediate future. To predict the future, you need to have a good grasp of the descriptive statistics to diagnose a business process. Lastly, the **Garbage-In-Garbage-Out** (**GIGO**) principle demands that analysis is only possible if we understand the collected data.

Collecting Data

The ultimate purpose of collecting data is to enable decisions that improve reality or reduce the risk of future adverse impacts. *Chapter 2, Good Data Science* discussed the importance of understanding the relationship between data and the reality it describes. This relationship is the essence of domain knowledge. Professionals in their respective domains are trained and experienced with measuring the reality they manage. *Chapter 2, Good Data Science* described some of the differences in measurement between the two domains.

The literature often distinguishes between raw data and processed data as the main ingredients of analysis. The idea that data can be raw and natural is deceiving. There is no such thing as raw data, because every time we collect information from a physical or social process, we need to decide how the data is collected. These decisions are always informed by assumptions about what this reality looks like before we see the data. We cannot measure anything if we don't know what it is.

In addition to these assumptions, we also need to choose which aspects of a process to measure. Every dataset is only a sample of reality informed by our assumptions. No amount of information will ever adequately describe the physical or social reality that we want to manage. All data collection is a process of compromise and assumptions. Understanding these assumptions and limitations is an essential step toward creating value.

The importance of the quality of the data cannot be understated. The GIGO principle is inescapable, even when using the most sophisticated machine learning algorithms. Understanding the quality of data requires subject-matter expertise and mathematical skills. The GIGO principle underwrites the importance of subject-matter experts who understand the flow of data from its creation to the point of analysis.

Data is always collected and stored to manage a business process. When a customer calls to lodge a complaint, the operator records this information to facilitate the customer's experience. When a treatment plant measures tank levels, the control system uses this information to decide when to run the filters to ensure the town does not run out of water. All data is used at or near the time of its creation. After the process has completed, it becomes dark data. This dramatic name does not do justice to the data and makes it seem like servers are full of useless bits and bytes. The data was, however, useful when it was generated and is merely waiting to be recycled.

Much of data science involves recycling this information to create additional value. In the case of a customer service process, we might analyze whether complaints cluster within a region. For the treatment plant, we can use this data to assess the performance of the plant to help us optimize energy consumption. Since the data revolution, more data is generated, used and archived than ever before. One of the powers of data science is to reuse this resource to gain additional insight to improve performance. A data scientist or business analyst is like an archaeologist who digs through electronic archives to make sense of the past to influence the future.

The salient point is that data is rarely collected for the purpose it was initially intended. This means that all data needs to be transformed into a format that is suitable to achieve the objectives of the project. Cleaning data is the least exciting activity of data science, but it often requires much of the available resources. The informal terms used in the industry for cleaning data are wrangling, munching or data jujitsu. These not so positive references illustrate the effort and frustration associated with cleaning data.

Reality is fickle which means that we never have access to all possible data about our variable of interest. People filling out a survey might not want to answer all questions due to privacy fears, survey fatigue or short attention spans. The technology used to collect data is never perfect, and physical measurements are often missing for various reasons.

Missing data needs to be managed by either imputing the gaps with estimated values or by removing parts of the sample. When only a few data points are missing, statistical methods can fill the gaps using various methods. Simple techniques, such as replacing missing data with the previous value or the mean, to more complex procedures that use machine learning, minimize the amount of missing data. When large chunks of data in surveys are missing, subjects with a low percentage of responses should be removed from the sample. Preventing GIGO syndrome means that the data scientist first needs to remove the garbage from the dataset. The most suitable method to manage missing data depends on the reasons it was missing and the impact of the missing points.

The data revolution has spawned the phenomenon of big data, briefly mentioned in *Sound Data Science section*. The issues regarding big data are mainly technical in nature, concerning storing, managing and analyzing this data. Accessing and analyzing billions of records requires specialized techniques, which are not relevant in small sets of data.

Besides its volume, big data is characterized by three other properties starting with the letter V. Big data has a lot of variety compared to traditional sources. The databases of quintessential big data organizations such as Google and Facebook contain information about a wide range of behaviors of its users. This data provides a digital fingerprint of our online lives, from the music we play to our network of friends.

Thirdly, big data has a very high velocity, resulting in many measurement points in a short period. This high velocity contrasts with the traditional sampling methods that only collect information every so many minutes, hours, or even days.

Lastly, big data has a high level of veracity. Traditional data sources about human behavior ask people what they feel or what they might do in the future. This approach has a low level of veracity because they are indirect measurements of behavior. Big data has a high level of reliability because it measures actual conduct.

The combination of this high volume, great variety, and high levels of velocity veracity is what gives big data its enormous power. At no point in human history have we had access to detailed information about our behavioral patterns. Most datasets used in organizations are, however, not big data.

Big data provides previously impossible opportunities for organizations that can generate this type of information. A dataset does not, however, must be big to create business value. Whether a dataset falls into the category of big data is not a concern from a strategic perspective but merely a technical problem. The main purpose of collecting evidence is to ensure that the information helps the organization to make evidence-based decisions. The same principles apply to all sources of data, big and small.

Descriptive Statistics

The first step in any analytical process is to describe the data under consideration. **Descriptive statistics** are methods, such as the average, median, range, standard deviation, and so on, that summarize a dataset. Business intelligence and exploratory analysis are the most common uses of descriptive statistics.

Descriptive statistics are the rear-view mirror of management. Most performance reports consist of large volumes of tables and graphs that report on what happened in the previous reporting period. Business reporting is often viewed as a lowly aspect of data science because you need to look through the windshield to drive a car, and not just look through the rear-view mirror. More crudely, some say that traditional performance reporting is like counting the dead after the battle has been fought.

Although this analogy might seem a compelling argument to ditch the traditional business report, it does not negate the importance of a rear-view mirror. The car analogy is also logically invalid because what we see through the windscreen is not the future, but the present. Business processes use data from the present through monitoring, and performance reporting teaches us about the past to learn to create a better future. Descriptive statistics are not an enough condition for becoming a data-driven organization but are nevertheless a necessary condition. Descriptive statistics are the unavoidable first step toward more complex analysis.

Business Reporting

When developing a business report, managers need to make two decisions. Firstly, they need to decide which performance indicators are important enough to include in the business report. The second decision is how to present this information so that readers of the report draw valid conclusions. Both choices require balancing various considerations. Choosing which performance indicators to include in a performance report is a fine art that needs to balance the requirements of completeness and consistency. Developing a performance dashboard is an iterative process where the measures are continuously fine-tuned.

The famous words of former General Electric CEO Jack Welch are frequently touted in boardrooms around the globe: "What you measure is what you get". (*Welch, J. (2001). Straight from the Gut. Warmer Books.*) This phrase is used so often that it has the status of a business axiom, the truth of which cannot be doubted. This rule suggests that the more you measure, the better you can control the destiny of your organization. Welch seems to warn us that any process missing from the business report is doomed to fail.

These are wise words, but measuring too many variables often leads to confusion, instead of enlightenment. It seems that the managers who use these words did not read the whole of Welch's book. Welch also moderates his insistence on measurement and writes that "too often we measure everything and understand nothing". It seems that business reporting hides a paradox.

No matter how many KPIs or other parameters you measure, a performance measurement system will never be both complete and consistent. This means that adding more and more traffic lights, graphs, maps and other elements to a dashboard increases the risk of confusion and inconsistency. The reverse side of this problem is that a minimalist dashboard of consistent descriptive statistics will be incomplete, because not everything of interest will be measured. (*Prevos, P. (2012). The incompleteness theorem of performance measurement in service delivery. In World Business Capability Congress. Auckland: Centre for Organizational Excellence Research (COER)*)

Once an analyst selects the ideal set of performance indicators, they decide how to communicate these to management. Many methods and tools enable reporting descriptive statistics. At the lowest level, we can display the information in a table so that users can explore the data for themselves. While this method provides excellent transparency, it leaves users to develop their own story about the information.

Conditional formatting to highlight some of the salient information enhances the tables but is not an ideal way to communicate data. Data visualization, as discussed in *Chapter 2, Good Data Science*, is a much more effective method to tell a story with data than tables. Best practice is to show the visualization and provide access to the graphed data in a table to promote full reproducibility and increase trust.

Diagnostics

Most analytical projects involve diagnosis, which is the process of finding causal or logical relationships between variables. Analyzing data uses mathematical transformations to find and validate relationships between variables. We might need to know whether complaints are clustered in a certain region of a service area or find the most likely cause of those complaints by relating it to other operational data.

This description implies that visualizing data to show a distribution or compare two or more variables is strictly speaking not analyzing anything. Descriptive statistics in most performance reports reduces the data to fewer numbers, but strictly speaking, does not add any information to the dataset. The average of a set of numbers or a trend line is already within the numbers. The defining property of diagnosis or analysis is that the cleaned data is transformed to reveal new information. An analysis shows us something that is not apparent from the data itself by combining and processing the information.

The analytical toolbox to find causal and logical relationships is vast and contains many different approaches to creating new knowledge. These methods cover a multitude of numerical techniques. Regression helps to find simple patterns; principal component analysis simplifies the data or Monte Carlo simulations to manage uncertainty. To comprehensively discuss the available methods is outside the scope of this book, as the literature on this topic is extensive.

Each domain of knowledge has its own specific methods to analyze information. Engineers often use calculus and linear algebra to solve problems. Marketers can use techniques such as **Partial-Least Square** modelling to measure latent variables to understand what their customers need and want. Economists have developed specialized econometrics to manage financial resources. Every field of human endeavor has developed their own mathematical perspective of the world.

Qualitative Data Science

Most analysis focuses on numerical or quantitative methods, but there is also value in analyzing qualitative information. Qualitative analysis is often seen as being less valuable than working with numbers because it is considered subjective. This subjectivity is not a value judgement of qualitative methods but an inherent issue in social science. Social scientists have developed methods to manage this subjectivity by combining qualitative and quantitative methods of analysis.

Computer-Assisted Qualitative Data Analysis is an emerging field of computing that helps researchers to manage large amounts of qualitative information using methods that minimize bias. These software packages help to manage transcriptions of interviews or focus groups, open-ended survey questions, social media or other forms of text. These types of analysis require the researcher first to untangle the texts and assign labels, codes or categories to them. Once the data is processed by the researcher, the computer assists in analyzing the relationships numerically. Techniques such as **Grounded Theory** or content analysis provide a systematic approach to extracting value from qualitative data.

Other qualitative techniques involve the automated analysis of texts and images. **Sentiment Analysis** is a useful technique to assess whether the sentiment of a section of text is positive, neutral or negative. Most of these methods rely on dictionaries of pre-classified words. The algorithm counts their occurrence, which determines whether the sentiment is positive or negative. For example, the word great would count toward a positive sentiment, while the word cheesy expresses a negative sentiment. The main problem with this technique is that many words in the English language are homographs, which are words that are spelled the same way, but have a different meaning. The word lead in context of water supply is usually negative, but the word lead in a business context could express a positive sentiment.

Other automated text analysis techniques use numerical methods to look for correlations between words. These text analysis methods are useful to make sense of a large amount of text without having to read each word. These methods reduce bias in analyzing qualitative information, but the output of such methods still needs to be interpreted by the researcher. None of these methods can, however, extract meaning from a text in the same way as a human would.

Predicting the Future

Predicting the future has been one of humanity's primary quests for millennia. Forces beyond our direct control influence our lives, and predictions allow us to control the ever-changing world around us to minimize risks to our lives. Before the age of enlightenment, humanity tried to grasp the unpredictability of existence with divination. They studied the movement of stars, animal entrails, tea leaves, and many other things to learn about their fate.

Since the scientific revolution, we no longer look at the stars, study tea leaves, or disembowel animals. Quantitative science is the most successful form of divination ever invented. Many methods are available to predict the future, from a simple linear regression model to more complex random forests and neural networks that are available to connect the past with the future.

Organizations that seek to reap the rewards of data science are often motivated by the capabilities of machine learning and other advanced techniques. Being able to predict possible futures allows a manager to assess whether this future is desirable. If this is not the case, then managers adjust current practice to create the desired future. If a retail store can predict whether consumers are likely to purchase a product because of their lifestyle preferences, then they can target them in their marketing communication to rattle their cage. If an engineer can predict that a piece of equipment is likely to fail soon, then it can be replaced to avoid problems.

Predictive analysis uses information about the past and uses logic to determine a possible future state of the variables in the model. A water utility can, for example, develop a predictive model to estimate the amount of water that their customers use on a given day using their property size, affluence, weather, and so on. A retailer could develop a predictive model of the amount of store traffic as a function of advertising, public holidays, sales, location, and whatever else might be predictive of this behavior.

All reliable methods to predict the future use information from the past, combined with a specified logic to estimate what could happen next. This future only eventuates when all boundary conditions under which this prediction was cast remain the same. No mathematical model can predict the future – it can only provide insight into possible futures. The purpose of predicting these possible futures is to determine the best cause of action to create the desired future.

This section provides a brief overview of predictive methods. The book Predictive Analysis, by Eric Siegel, provides a comprehensive introduction into methods to predict the future. (E. (2016). *Predictive Analytics: The Power to Predict Who Will Click, Buy, Lie, or Die. Wiley).*

The various methods to describe plausible futures consist of two approaches, each based on different assumptions. Traditional methods follow the scientific process of experimentally verifying hypotheses. Machine learning is entirely different in that it does not use a hypothesis.

Traditional Predictive Methods

The scientific method is the traditional process to develop a predictive model of the world as shown in *Figure* 3.2. This is a circular process that describes an ongoing improvement in our understanding of the world (*Lee, N., & Lings, I. (2008). Doing Business Research: A Guide to Theory and Practice. London: SAGE).*

A manager observes the process they are interested in through descriptive statistics. Any anomalies that appear in the latest corporate dashboard lead to new questions about what caused the deviation from the desired outcome.

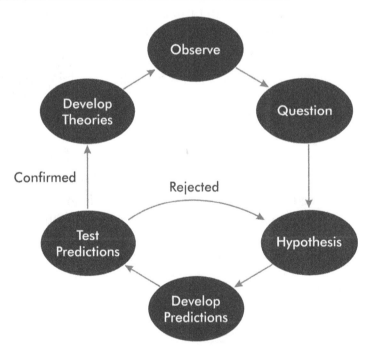

Figure 3.2: The process of science

The traditional method to answer these questions starts with a hypothesis, which is a statement that can be confirmed or rejected. A manager might want to know why sales are trending downwards and hypothesize that a series of scorching days demotivated consumers to visit the outdoor shopping center caused the decline. The analyst then develops a method to either verify or reject the hypothesis, which increases our knowledge about the world. The store manager can then use this knowledge to decide whether it is worth moving to an air-conditioned shopping mall to maximize store traffic.

Some scientific processes lead to generalized knowledge of the world in the form of a theory. The scientific view of a theory is entirely different from the common sense understanding of something that might or might not be true. A theory is a confirmed relationship between variables measured. For example, the theory of gravity, which explains the forces between two objects, reliably predicts the motion of objects.

Scientists have developed thousands of theories to help us explain the world. Scientific theories are a convenient way to predict and thus control the future. Most theories that predict the future are about the physical world. There are almost no traditional theories in the scientific sense that allow us to predict human behavior, neither individually nor collectively, reliably.

Once these theories are accepted and used, further observations will raise new questions, and the same process is followed again. The critical aspect to realize is that the insight of the researcher guides this process. Formulating a reasonable hypothesis requires a deep understanding of the subject matter under consideration.

The outcome of the scientific process is in many cases a formula that describes the relationship between different states of reality. Scientists prefer elegant theories. An elegant theory can be written down in a relatively simple formula. The famous physicist Stephen Hawking wrote in his inspiring book, A *Brief History of Time*, that his dream was to one day have a formula that describes everything in the Universe that fits on a t-shirt.

Machine Learning

Machine learning is without a doubt the poster child of data science. This popular technique possibly promises more than it can deliver. Machines cannot learn anything. Machine learning is a group of complex algorithms that convert the input into output by recognizing patterns in data. The term was coined by Arthur Samuel at IBM in 1959 to promote their capabilities in software development (*Burkov, A. (2019). The Hundred-Page Machine Learning Book. LeanPub*).

Machine learning is a branch of **Artificial Intelligence** (AI). The set of algorithms that are classified as machine learning are part of the AI toolkit but are not the only ways to mimic human reasoning.

Machine learning works differently to traditional prediction methods because it is the machines themselves that create the equations, not the researcher. The family tree of machine learning has three main branches: supervised and unsupervised methods, and reinforcement learning, as shown in *Figure 3.3*.

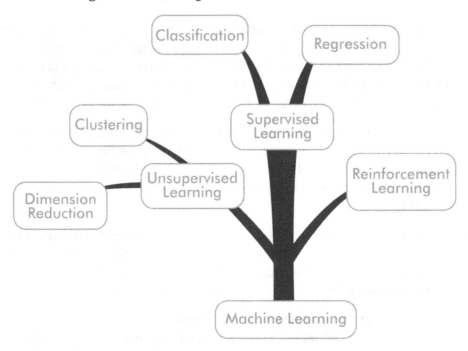

Figure 3.3: Overview of machine learning methods

In supervised methods, the algorithm is provided with a set of training data with known relationships. When, for example, wanting to predict how much a viewer will like a movie, the training data consists of verified information about what movies people have watched and how they rated them. A supervised algorithm analyses the training data to discover patterns so that we can predict how likely a viewer will enjoy a new movie. Supervised learning can classify data in groups, or it can regress data to find relationships between variables.

Recognizing cats in images is an example of classification. The algorithm is presented with thousands of labelled images, some of which contain a cat, and some don't. The algorithm is taught how to recognize a cat using these examples. Supervised learning is like how humans learn to classify the world. As children, we are provided with examples of cats by our parents, and after we've acquired the skill of recognizing cats, we can independently classify furry animals as either a cat or something else.

Regression analysis finds relationships between numerical or categorical variables using independent variables and known dependent variables. The independent variables are the causes of the dependent variable. We might know that the likelihood of rain relates to temperature and moisture content of the air. This mathematical relationship is then used to predict the weather, estimate the life expectancy of people or assets, and anything else that occurs over time.

One of the most important considerations of supervised machine learning is the size of the training dataset. When this set is too large, the algorithm will find patterns where they don't exist, which is called over-fitting. When the dataset is not large enough, it will be unable to find any patterns. Fine-tuning a predictive algorithm to deliver reliable predictions is a craft that requires great insight into the algorithm.

Unsupervised methods operate without labelled examples. These algorithms trawl through the data to find patterns. Clustering method detects groups of data in multi-dimensional data. This technique is useful to segment customers using sets of characteristics. Segmenting customers helps organizations to target their marketing. Unsupervised methods can also reduce the dimensionality of data. These techniques are helpful to discover otherwise invisible aspects of the data. Factor analysis and structural equation modelling are examples of methods to analyze social surveys and find underlying patterns.

The output of these machine learning methods is very different from traditional analysis. While scientists wear t-shirts with elegant formulas, the outcomes of machine learning are often utterly incomprehensible to humans. This aspect of machine learning can be a problem as professionals hesitate to accept the outcomes of the algorithm if they can't see or understand the logic that the machine uses to achieve its results. This problem highlights the need for data science education among all professionals and not only specialists.

The third method, **reinforcement learning** is a technique that is used in prescriptive analysis, which is the topic of the next section.

Prescribing Action

The last step in the continuum is where machines take over our world, and human beings can relax and be served by their robot slaves. This vision might seem science fiction, but automated processes have been part of our lives for many decades.

Industrial systems need to be controlled by operators to ensure that they produce the outcomes we need. When, for example, a tank of chemicals reaches a certain low level, a pump needs to be started to fill it again, and the operator needs to monitor the tank. Manual systems require a human operator to review measurements of the state of the system and take appropriate action. The first level of automation uses a control loop to measure the level of the tank and an automated valve.

Almost all contemporary manufacturing processes use these first-generation control loops. The problem with these systems is that they rely on preset conditions that might not be suitable when external circumstances change. Traditional control systems measure the present and act when the measured value starts to trend toward a set value. In effect, a control system consists of a network of if-then statements to manage all the standard conditions. When the environment deviates from the boundary conditions that the system was designed to operate, the system will fail.

Machine learning can enhance traditional control systems by simulating the environment instead of relying on limited boundary conditions. Reinforcement learning uses the principles of game theory to find solutions that maximize outcomes. This method uses a virtual carrot and stick as the algorithm finds a way to optimize predefined conditions. Reinforcement learning is very close to the way organisms learn. When an animal, human or otherwise, behaves in a certain way is positively rewarded, the behavior will be reinforced and repeated in similar future situations.

This method simulates the environment it wants to control and simulates millions of possible decisions to determine the most optimal choice. This method has been insanely successful in playing complex board games, such as Go and chess. Reinforcement learning is ideal for games, because reality can be simulated perfectly. Deploying these methods in real-world systems is much more complicated, because simulating a natural or social environment is much more complicated than the ideal environment of a board game.

Toward a Data-Driven Organization

The data science continuum provides a strategic map for organizations that seek to become more data-driven. Each of the steps in the continuum is equally important to the next level because these higher levels of complexity cannot be achieved without embracing the lower levels. The most important aspect of the data science continuum is that it summarizes an evolutionary approach toward becoming a data-driven organization. As an organization evolves toward more complex forms of data science, the earlier stages don't become vestigial appendices but remain an integral part of the data science strategy. All parts of this model are of equal relative value.

Being data-driven is, however, more than a process of increasing complexity. Evidence-based management requires the people within the organization to be data literate and work together toward a common goal. The systematic aspect of data science needs a formalized process to ensure sound outcomes. The increased complexity of the analytical methods also requires an investment in better tools and data infrastructure. *Chapter 4, The Data-Driven Organization* of this book reflects on the non-technical aspects of data science and discusses the people, process, and systems required to become a data-driven organization. The book closes with a reflection on the limitations of data science from a mathematical and ethical perspective.

The Data-Driven Organization

Introduction

The previous two chapters describe some of the technical aspects to consider when implementing data science in an organization. Merely focusing on the technicalities of analyzing data is, however, not enough to create value for an organization. A data science manager needs to manage people, systems, and process to develop a data-driven organization.

Decision makers sometimes ignore even the most useful and aesthetic visualizations, even when the analysis is sound. Data science using best practices, as described in *Chapter 2, Good Data Science*, is only the starting point for creating a value-driven organization. A critical aspect of ensuring that managers use the results is to foster a data-driven culture, which requires managing people.

To enable data science to flourish, the organization needs to have a well-established suite of IT systems to store and analyze data and to present the results. A wide range of data science tools is available, each playing a different role in the analytics value chain.

Every data science project starts with a problem definition that is translated into data and code to define a solution. This problem is injected into the data vortex until a solution is found. The process of data science discusses the workflow of creating data products.

This final chapter discusses these three aspects of becoming a data-driven organization. To strategically implement data science requires aligning people, systems, and processes to optimize the value that can be extracted from the available information. The next three sections discuss these aspects of data science. This book closes with some deliberations about the theoretical and ethical limitations of data science.

People

When discussing the people related to a data-driven organization, we should not only mention the specialists that create the data products. The members of the data science team possess the competencies shown in the Conway diagram in *Figure* 1.3. They also need to be able to communicate the results of their work to colleagues or clients and convince them to implement the findings.

Data science does not only exclusively happen within the specialized team. Each data project has an internal or external customer that has a problem in need of an answer. The data science team and the users of their products work together to improve the organization. This implies that a data scientist needs to understand the basic principles of organizational behavior and change management and be a good communicator. In reverse, the recipients of data science need to have enough data literacy to understand how to interpret and use the results.

The Data Science Team

Contemporary folklore portrays the data scientist as the slightly socially awkward genius. The geek in the movies converts energy drinks and junk food into computer code and solves a complex problem with merely a few keystrokes. While much of data science relies on the talents of highly skilled individuals, a strategic approach to creating value from data is more teamwork than it is the domain of the lone genius. The ideal data science team combines all the skills and expertise needed to complete its task.

The Conway diagram visualizes the technical skills of the data science team. To be able to embed the results into the organization, data scientists need people skills in addition to technical competencies. These soft skills are not part of the Conway diagram because they are common to all professions. Their absence from the picture is no indication of their lesser importance. *Data Science Culture* discusses the cultural aspects of being data-driven.

From the fact that a data scientist requires well-developed competencies in writing code, it does not follow that the data science function naturally forms part of the Information Technology (IT) team. Writing code is traditionally seen as a competency of IT professionals. Anyone outside this group that wants to maximize the capabilities of the hardware and software they are provided is often labelled as 'shadow IT'.

Consultancy firm Gartner regularly releases predictions about how they perceive the future of computing. A few years ago, they suggested that a significant part of IT expenditure will occur outside the traditional lines of responsibility. *Gartner. (2011). Gartner Reveals Top Predictions for IT Organizations and Users for 2012 and Beyond (Press Release)*. As most functions become ever more reliant on digital technology, traditional IT skills are distributed around the organization. The idea that only IT professionals write code is indeed incorrect from a data science perspective, because developing a spreadsheet is not much different from developing software.

Centralizing all IT management in one team is like having the Human Resource (HR) manager conduct all performance reviews or be responsible for hiring all people in the company. Just like HR, information technology skills need to be decentralized to maximize the value we can extract from existing infrastructure.

The data science industry is frantically looking for so-called unicorns, which are people that have all three skills in the Conway diagram. The most effective way to achieve this ideal is to teach existing subject-matter experts to write code. This approach creates data scientists with domain knowledge and improves data literacy. Embracing the shadow IT ethos and distributing coding skills around the organization is one part of developing a data-driven organization.

Data science can be positioned in two ways within an organization. A team can be embedded within a product or service group, or it can be a dedicated team that services all parts of the organization. Smaller organizations will most likely have one specialized team that services the organization. A disadvantage of a centralized data science team is that it creates a distance between the operational managers and the data specialists, which complicates implementing the results. Larger organizations have a workload that is enough to justify more than one data science knowledge center. Data science competencies embedded with an operational team places them within the action, which allows them to respond rapidly to operational needs. The disadvantage of this method is that expertise is fragmented across the organization (*Caffo, Peng, & Leek (2018)*).

Data Science Consumers

The main hurdle for creating a data-driven organization is that not everybody fully understands the results of sophisticated analysis. Data scientists are responsible for producing aesthetic reports and visualizations to ensure that the user grasps the end-product. When professionals fail to understand the analysis, the results will be ignored, and they revert to their intuitive understanding of the problem.

Statistics can often be counter-intuitive, and some people have a low level of trust in the mathematical wizardry of the data scientist. Mark Twain popularized the phrase "Lies, damned lies, and statistics". The complexity of statistics makes it an ideal vehicle to use as a propaganda tool, which these days we call fake news. Lying with statistics is easy when the receiver has a low level of data literacy. (*Huff, D. (1985). How to Lie with Statistics (Reprint). Harmondsworth: Penguin Books*).

Unfortunately, the physical and social world are inherently stochastic in nature. In addition to this uncertainty, all measurements introduce a level of random error. Statistics are thus the most effective way to understand reality. We can never understand the world with arbitrary mathematical precision and can only rely on a statistical description. The most perfect knowledge of the world we can ever have is statistical. When statistics are appropriately applied, Mark Twain's phrase should be reversed: "truth, absolute truth, and statistics".

This fact places requirements on the consumers of the results of data science. Data literacy is an inherently mathematical skill, but unfortunately, many people have grown up fearing the most beautiful of all sciences. This does not imply that all employees need to do a mathematics course. The data scientist needs to create aesthetic products that require only a common sense understanding of the world. Unfortunately, this is only possible for the simplest of business problems.

Moving toward artificial intelligence is a fool's errand if we don't also invest in natural intelligence. Implementing a data science strategy requires an investment in professional development to increase data literacy. For complex data science to deliver value, the whole of the organization needs to be data literate at the appropriate level.

Data literacy is the ability to identify, locate, interpret and evaluate quantitative and qualitative information and communicate the results. The scope of data literacy envelopes the whole of the data science workflow described in *Process section*. The data literacy curriculum consists of several areas of competency.

Employees need to be able to source information and understand how data is governed. Employees undertaking analysis need to be versed in research skills and know how to manipulate data. The third aspect of data literacy are skills to interpret statistics. Visualizing information and presenting evidence to decision makers are the last two data competencies (*Australian Public Service Commission. (2018). Data literacy skills. Retrieved 2 March 2019, from*—https://www.apsc.gov.au/data-literacy-skills).

The extent to which employees need to have data competencies depends on their position within the organization. We expect a much higher level of data literacy from technical professionals than we would from administrative staff.

The reliance on electronic tools to interrogate data implies that data literacy goes together with digital literacy. Users need to be computer literate and able to use the various tools of the trade confidently. Contemporary business intelligence tools have simplified the level of skill required to extract and model multiple sets of data. Having digital skills in isolation of data skills can, however, lead to problems because users draw incorrect conclusions due to wrong methodologies or lack of validation, as discussed in *Conway's danger zone*.

Data science consumers are not only the colleagues of the data scientist or the clients of a consultant, but they are also the consumers of the products and services of the organization. Businesses and government agencies love to publish statistics to show their customers or the community how awesome they are. Communicating accurate statistics is an effective way to foster trust between the organization and its stakeholders. This method only works, however, when the targeted people have enough data literacy to understand the information. Most data communication is produced by highly intelligent professionals who find it difficult to understand the limitations of their less educated fellow citizens.

The European Union has published a framework for the digital competency of its citizens. This document recognizes the importance of digital literacy to maximize participation in society. This document discusses information literacy, the ability to communicate and collaborate, the ability to create digital content, digital safety, and problem-solving as its five areas of competency. (*Carretero, S., Vuorikari, R., Punie, Y., European Commission, & Joint Research Centre. (2017). DigComp 2.1 The Digital Competence Framework for Citizens with Eight Proficiency Levels and Examples of Use*).

Closing the data literacy gaps between data science and its consumers requires movement in two directions. Firstly, the analyst needs to be a great communicator and convey their message in convincing and straightforward language, as discussed in *Chapter 2, Good Data Science*. Secondly, the consumers of data science need to be educated to an enough level to help them navigate the complex world of statistics.

Data Science Culture

The data revolution has made some organizations realize that they are data-rich, but information-poor. Managers in these organizations realize that they hold large amounts of data that is only used once. The popularity of data science is to a large extent motivated by a desire to use this dark data and become more data-driven.

The most complicated aspect of implementing a data science strategy is to integrate the results of our analysis with every-day business activities. A data-driven organization is one where using information to solve problems forms part of its culture. On the surface, this can be achieved by updating the existing operating procedure to include analyzing data, but there is also a strong human component to this transition.

The hundreds of published definitions of culture illustrate the complexity of the concept of organizational culture. The main reason for this confusion is that culture is often defined in abstract terms for which there is no empirical way to study them. The most pragmatic and productive way to discuss culture is to examine its phenomena instead of trying to define its essence. A phenomenological approach investigates the visible aspects of a culture to learn something about the invisible dimensions.

The image in *Figure 4.1* uses the well-known iceberg analogy to list some of the visible and invisible phenomena of organizational culture. This model helps to explain what a data science culture means in practice, and how to recognize or create it. (*McShane, S., & Travaglione, T. (2005). Organizational Behavior on the Pacific Rim (Enhanced ed.). North Ryde N.S.W.: McGraw-Hill*).

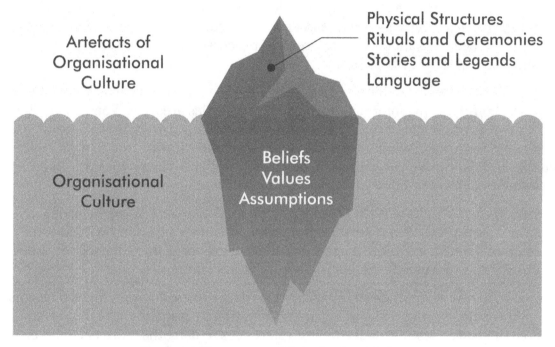

Figure 4.1: Phenomena of Organizational Culture.

Before we can say anything sensible about the data culture of an organization, we need to understand artefacts. An artefact is a visible expression of culture that can be observed, studied, and/or measured. A focus on the tangible aspects of culture also makes it easier to change them, because we can modify things we can measure.

The physical structures of an organization are the most concrete artefacts. The office is a physical structure that expresses the culture of an organization. Is the office a cubicle maze or does it provide an open and collaborative space to work in teams? The office is also a place to distribute communication through works of art and posters. A data-driven organization displays visualizations and other analytical results on walls or on the intranet to inform employees of exciting information.

An organization is like a tribe that has its own specific rituals and ceremonies. The word ritual is often reserved for a meaningless and repetitive activity. Rituals and ceremonies are not merely useless activities – they form an essential part of human social life. Also, outside the realm of religion, rituals are an indispensable tool that add structure to social life. The induction of new staff is an initiation ceremony that transforms a job applicant into an employee. This ritual provides a strong signal to the novice about the culture of their new place of work. A data-driven organization introduces the new employee to their relevant data structures and processes in order to obtain and analyze this information.

The stories and legends within an organization are the unwritten narratives that circle around the office during informal meetings. These stories are passed on and modified by the generations of employees. If an organization is data-driven, then at least some of these stories would include stories about data and how it was used to do something valuable. In a data-driven organization, employees not only communicate with data through formal reports, but they also refer to it in informal settings.

The last artefact of culture is the language of an organization. The language of employees, as expressed in reports, memos, emails, and so on, is a robust indicator of the extent to which data informs decisions. Business reports, investment proposals, and any other formal document should use data as its foundation.

To assess the extent to which an organization is data driven, you should become a part-time anthropologist who uses participant observation to evaluate these four artefacts of culture. The more these artefacts include references to data, the more data-driven an organization is.

The beliefs, values, and assumptions of an organizational culture are much harder to measure or observe than visible artefacts. Psychometric surveys can provide some insight, but in corporate settings, often, these tend to measure politically correct opinions, instead of the actual attitudes of employees. Employees often respond with what they believe should be the case, instead of what is the case.

The invisible aspect of organizational culture and the visible artefacts have a two-way causal relationship. The intangible elements of a culture influence how we behave and communicate, and the artefacts are thus a result of culture. This mechanism also works in the reverse direction in that the artefacts modify our beliefs, values, and attitudes.

The collective minds of employees around the world shudder when they hear managers utter the words culture change. Most cultural change programs fail because managers don't themselves display the values they aspire to. Changing the culture to some ideal that a manager reads about in an inspiring article is doomed to fail at the best of times.

Changing the values and beliefs of employees in an organization is extremely hard and often leads to resistance. Sending employees to development sessions to develop artificial values is, in most cases, not very productive. The easiest way to change an organizational culture is to improve the visible signs. The intangible aspects of culture will slowly but surely modify themselves to the messages embedded within the artefacts. The physical structures change the way employees interact with each other. As more new staff are recruited, the percentage of employees that undergo the new induction becomes greater. The more the formal and informal language of the organization includes references to data, the more it will become part of its culture.

A data-driven manager can change an organization by modifying the artefacts of the organizational culture and infusing them with reports and visualizations. The more the artefacts include references to data and analysis, the more the beliefs, values, and assumptions will become driven by data.

Systems

Just like any other profession, a data scientist needs a suitable set of tools to create value from data. A plethora of data science solutions is available on the market, many of which are open source software. Specialized tools exist for each aspect of the data science workflow.

There is no need to discuss the multitude of packages that are available. Many excellent websites review the various offerings. This section provides some thoughts on the use of spreadsheets versus writing code and business intelligence platforms.

Spreadsheets are a versatile tool to analyze data that has proliferated into almost every aspect of business. This universal tool is, however, not very suitable to undertake complex data science. One of the perceived advantages of spreadsheets is that they contain the data, the code and the output in one convenient file. This convenience comes at a price as it reduces the soundness of the analysis. Anyone who ever had the displeasure of reverse-engineering a spreadsheet will understand the limitations of spreadsheets. In spreadsheets, it is not immediately clear which cell is the result of another cell and which ones are original data. Many organizations use spreadsheets as a single source of truth for corporate data, which should be avoided if the information needs to be shared. The data science best practice is to separate data, code, and output.

As mentioned previously, the best way to breed data science unicorns is to teach subject-matter experts to write analytical code. Writing code such as R or Python is like writing an instruction manual on how to analyze data. Anyone who understands the language will be able to know how you derived your conclusions. Modern data science languages can generate print-quality visualizations and can output results in many formats, including a spreadsheet or a stand-alone application.

The gold standard for data science coding is literate programming. This technique combines the code with prose to enable the algorithm to be fully understood. All computing languages include the ability to add comments. Literate programming is a further evolution of this technique. The results of literate programming are most commonly a report or a deck of presentation slides.

Each language has its own methods to combine text with code. **RMarkdown**, **Jupyter Notebooks**, and **Org Mode** are popular systems to undertake literate programming. Once the code is written, at the push of a button the computer generates a new report with updated statistics and graphics. You can either choose to include or exclude the code from the result, depending on the expertise of the reader.

Lastly, business intelligence tools are useful to disseminate the results of a data science project but are not very useful to undertake detailed analysis. A platform such as **Power BI** is a great system to visualize the result of analysis because it provides very flexible ways to slice-and-dice the data and visualize results. The analytical capabilities of the platform are not very high but can be amended by inserting code in Python or R to complement its capabilities.

Process

Chapter 2, Good Data Science, mentioned the requirement for governance in data science to ensure the outcomes of projects are sound. The process of creating value from data follows an iterative workflow that works from raw data to a finished project. (*Wickham, H., & Grolemund, G. (2016). R for data science: Import, Tidy, Transform, Visualize, and Model Data Sebastopol, CA: O'Reilly. Available at*—https://r4ds.had.co.nz/). The workflow starts with defining a problem that needs solving as shown in *Figure 4.2*. The next step involves loading and transforming the data into a format that is suitable for the required analysis. The data science workflow contains a loop that consists of exploration, modelling, and reflection, which is repeated until the problem is solved or is shown to be unsolvable.

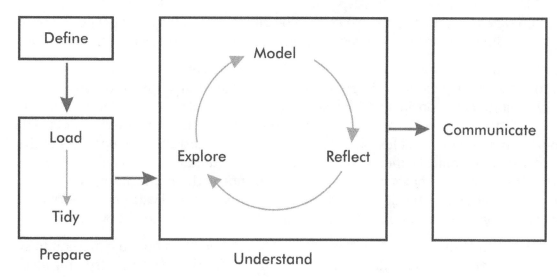

Figure 4.2: Data science workflow

The workflow for a data project is independent of the aspect of the data science continuum under consideration. The same principles apply to every type of analysis. For larger projects, formal project management methods are advisable to control time, budget, and quality.

The following sections describe some salient aspects of each of the three phases in the data science workflow and present a case study about reporting water quality to a board of directors. (*Prevos, P. (2015). Visualising water quality: A graphical index for drinking water system performance. In OzWater. Adelaide: Australian Water Association*).

Define

The first step of a data science project is to define the problem. This first step describes the problem under consideration and the desired future state. The problem definition should not make specific reference to available data or possible methods but be limited to the issue at hand. An organization could seek to optimize production facilities, reduce energy consumption, monitor effectiveness, understand customers, and so on. A concise problem definition is necessary to ensure that a project does not deviate from its original purpose, or that it is cancelled when it becomes apparent that the problem cannot be solved.

The outcome of a data science project can be either actionable intelligence or improved understanding of a business process, as discussed in *the Useful Data Science section*.

The problem definition opens with a description of the current situation and clearly identifies which aspect needs improvement or more profound understanding. The problem statement concludes with a summary of the ideal situation. For example, a water utility reports water quality results to the board of directors every month. The report contains a lot of tables with results of laboratory testing. The members of the board are not technical experts and don't fully understand what they mean. Another section of the report shows water quality complaints, without indicating how they relate to water quality results. The board has asked for a visualization to report water quality performance that combines the available data in one succinct overview.

The definition of the project concludes with a description of a possible method to solve the problem and the data sources needed to implement the solution. Assuming all the required sources of data are available, the analytical process can commence.

For the case study, the analyst decided to use a performance index for each of the different aspects of the water supply system. A water quality index is a dimensionless number that reflects the level of performance compared to an ideal situation.

Prepare

The available data needs to be loaded and wrangled into the required format before any analysis can take place. Influential data scientist Hadley Wickham refers to this process as tidying data (*Wickham and Grolemund (2016)*). Anecdotally, this phase of the project could consume up to 80% of the work effort, depending on the difference between the available data and the required data.

A best practice in data science is to record every dataset that is considered for the project. A data book records every field extracted from a source to ensure the context in which the data was created is understood.

Source	Source	Availability
Catchment	Paper records	Intermittent
Treatment plant	SCADA	Continuous
Network	Laboratory	Weekly
Customer experience	Complaints	Daily
Regulation	Issues register	Intermittent

Figure 4.3: Data science case study: available data

For the water utility case study, several data sources are available, as shown in the table. The data scientist needs to decide which of these sources solves the problem. In this example, the data from the catchments is only available on paper, which makes it difficult to analyze it algorithmically. A separate project would be required to convert this source to electronic data. Other data sources are available electronically and can be used for the project.

Understand

Once the data is available in a tidy format, the process of understanding the data can commence. The analytical phase consists of a three-stage loop, the data vortex, which is repeated until the required results are achieved, or evidence becomes available that the objectives cannot be met. These three stages are explore, model, and reflect.

- **Explore**: The best method to start analyzing data is to explore the data to understand its relationship to reality. Generating descriptive statistics such as averages, ranges, and correlations provides a quick insight into the data. Relying on numerical analysis alone can, however, be deceptive, because very different sets of data can result in the same values. Justin Matejka and George Fitzmaurice from AutoDesk demonstrated how very different sets of data can have almost the same summary statistics. Each of these six visualizations shows that these sets of data have very different patterns. When, however, analyzing this data without visualizing it, the mean values of x and y, and their correlations, are almost the same for all six subsets. In their paper, they presented an algorithm that generates every possible pattern with the same summary values, six of which are shown in the illustration. (*Matejka, J., & Fitzmaurice, G. (2017). Same Stats, Different Graphs: Generating Datasets with Varied Appearance and Identical Statistics through Simulated Annealing. In Proceedings of the 2017 CHI Conference on Human Factors in Computing Systems - CHI '17 (pp. 1290–1294). Denver, Colorado, USA: ACM Press–* https://doi.org/10.1145/3025453.3025912).

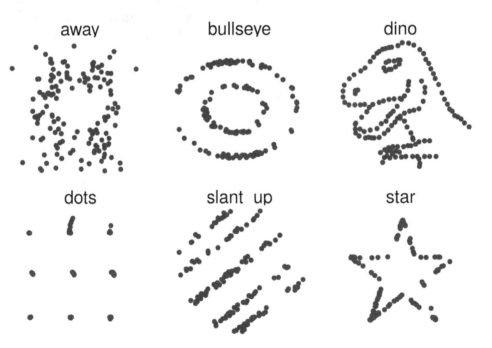

Figure 4.4: Six patterns with very similar summary statistics

Another reason to use visualizations to explore data is to reveal **anomalies**, such as unnatural **spikes** or **outliers**. A sudden increase and decrease in physical measurements are often caused by issues with measurement or data transmission instead of actual changes. These spikes need to be removed to ensure the analysis is reliable. Anomalies in social data such as surveys could be subjects that provide the same question to all answers, discussed in the previous chapter.

Detecting outliers and anomalies and removing these from a dataset increases the reliability of the analysis. Not all anomalies in a dataset are necessarily suspicious, and care should be taken before removing data. The reasons for removing any anomalous data should be documented so that the analyses remain reproducible.

The exploratory analysis in the case study involved generating time series charts for all relevant data to understand the statistical distributions. What are the maximum and minimum values? How variable are these observations? These, and other basic statistics, provide insight into the shape of the data used.

- **Model**: After the analyst has a good grasp of the variables under consideration, the actual analysis can commence. Modelling involves transforming the problem statement into mathematics and code, as described in *Chapter 3, Strategic Data Science*. Every model of the world is bounded by the assumptions contained within it. Statistician George Box is famous for stating that "all models of reality are wrong, but some are useful". Since data science is all about deriving meaningful insights from our data to take calculated business decisions, a useful model is all we need. When modelling the data, the original research question always needs to be kept in mind. Exploring and analyzing data without a specific purpose can quickly lead to wrong conclusions. Just because two variables correlate does not imply that there is a logical relationship. A clearly defined problem statement and method prevent data dredging. The availability of data and the ease of extracting this information makes it easy for anyone to find relationships between different sources of information. A good general rule when analyzing data is to distrust your method when you can confirm your hypothesis easily. If this is the case, using triangulation through a different method helps to verify the results. The modelling in this case study involved developing a demerit point system. Perfect water quality is almost always defined by lower and upper limits for a parameter. Perfect water has no color, has a minimum level of chlorine, and so on. This information forms the basis of a points system. When, for example, water has a measurable color, the index is reduced by a certain amount of points. A decision rule was designed for each parameter in the model.

- **Reflect**: Before the results of an analysis can be communicated, domain experts need to review the outcomes to ensure they make sense and indeed solve the problem stated in the definition. The reflection phase should also include the customer to ensure that the problem statement is being solved to their satisfaction. Visualization is a quick method to establish whether the outcomes make sense by revealing apparent patterns. Another powerful technique to reflect on the results is sensitivity analysis. This technique involves changing some of the assumptions to test the model responds as expected. Mathematical models are often complex where the relationship between variables is not clearly understood. Sensitivity analysis helps to understand these relationships by using extreme for certain variables and then observe the effect on the model. Concerning the case study, the modelling required a lot of reflection on the chosen model and required many iterations of the data vortex. Developing a performance index is a balancing act to ensure each parameter is appropriately weighted. The purpose of the index was to provide the board with salient information so they can ask targeted questions during meetings. The reflection phase always needs to reflect on the purpose and ensure it is achieved.

Communicate

The last, and arguably the hardest, phase of a data science project is to communicate the results to the users. In most cases, the users of the data product are not specialists with a deep understanding of data and mathematics. The difference in skills between the data scientist and the user of their products requires careful communication of the results.

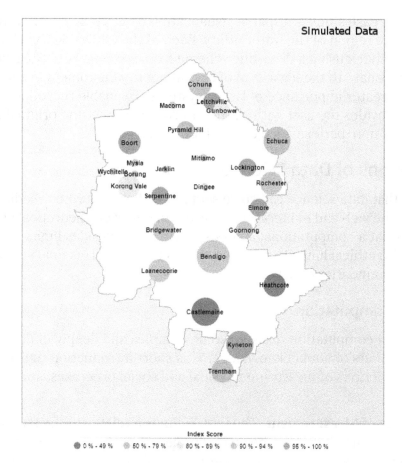

Figure 4.5: Water System Index visualization

Detailed reports and visualizations need to not only provide an accurate description of the outcomes, but they also need to be able to convince the reader. The most critical aspect of successfully communicating the solution to the problem is to ensure that the consumers of the results understand them and are willing to use them to solve the problem. As much as data science is a systematic process, it is also a cultural process that involves managing the internal change in the organization, as discussed in *Define* section.

The result of this case study is a spatial visualization of all the water treatment plants within the service region of the water utility. Each of the circles on the chart visualizes the result of the index using a diverging scheme from red to green. The size of the circle is proportionate to the logarithm of the number of customers in each town to emphasize the greater importance of larger systems. To enable reproducibility, clicking on the circles provides the user with all the internal workings and original data so that the root cause of non-performance can be identified.

The Limitations of Data Science

The problems that data science can solve seem to be limitless when reading some of the articles on the web and in literature. There are, however, theoretical and practical limitations to what a computational analysis can achieve. Besides limits to what we can do, there are also ethical limits to what we should be doing. This final section reflects on some of the boundaries of data science.

The Limits of Computation

The limitations of computation relate to some complex and deeply philosophical issues concerning the limits of human knowledge. This short introduction to this problem looks at the restrictions of measuring physical and social processes, and the limitations of algorithms.

- **Limitations of Measurement**: The first limitation relates to the fact that our collection of data will always be an incomplete description of reality. In a physical system, choose which points to measure, at which frequency, by which method, and so on. We need to make a lot of choices before we can access data. Even more so with social data, all our measurements are only indirect expressions of the reality we seek to explain.

  As discussed in the *Sound Data Science* section, measurements are never a perfect copy of the reality it describes. There is no such thing as raw data because all measurement uses assumptions about the reality it represents. These limitations of data restrict what we can know about the future. Predictions all use the same principle to achieve a result. Patterns in the data about the past are used to extrapolate the current situation to a plausible future. As our data is, however, always incomplete, these models will quickly sharply produce.

Complex systems such as the weather will never be predicted over the long term due to the inherent gaps in data from a spatial perspective. Dynamic systems are highly dependent on initial conditions. A slight measurement error will be amplified over time and render long-term predictions impossible. Social systems are even more complicated than dynamic physical systems. Even though big data is quite successful at modelling aspects of human behavior, it is incapable of providing a broad model of our actions. Amazon might be able to predict which brand of laptop I am most likely to purchase, but there is not much more they can do with the information I volunteer to them. Although it might be possible to measure everything in principle, the simple cost of doing so is prohibitive. Certain aspects of reality are intrinsically hard to measure. A seemingly simple parameter, such as the presence of pathogens, takes a lot of effort to determine. Even if we succeed in measuring vast amounts of data, the computational cost of processing this information needs to reasonably relate to the anticipated benefits.

- **Limitations of Algorithms**: Computational methods to solve problems are potent methods to answer questions that, not long ago, we didn't even dare to ask. There are, however, specific problems that even the smartest algorithms cannot solve. An example of an intrinsically hard problem is the travelling salesman. An organization has salespeople that need to visit many cities. Salespeople seek to minimize the amount of time they spend on the road and thus they need to know the shortest possible routes between all towns. Although some algorithms exist for this problem, they only provide estimates. To determine the actual shortest path requires an astronomical amount of computing time. If the problem contains a high enough number of cities, the computational time necessary to find the solution could be longer than the age of the Universe.

- **Beyond the Limitations**: Some of these limitations might be circumvented in the future, but some of these issues are fundamental problems without a solution. The problem of incomplete information will never be fully resolved as the practical difficulties are insurmountable. The power of computers has grown exponentially for the past fifty years, and quantum computing will be the next leap in capabilities. The problems with algorithmic complexity will, however, not be resolved by even the fastest quantum computer imaginable. The limitations listed in this section are profound and, as far as we can gather from our current perspective, are unassailable. These limitations are not stopping us from doing a lot more with data than most organizations can achieve at this moment. Even within the constraints of solving problems with computational analysis, there are still many things we can accomplish with algorithms. The limitations of data science not only extend to what data science could do, but also to what it ought to do. Analyzing data is an inherently human activity, which means it always has an ethical dimension. The ethics of data science places limitations on what info we collect, how we disseminate this information, and what we do with the results of an analysis.

Ethical Data Science

Technology gives humanity capabilities far beyond what we are naturally capable of. Machines make us stronger, but they can cause physical damage to people and the environment. Computers make us smarter, but they can also cause social damage. With this great power comes great responsibility. *Donald Knuth* is one of the original computer gurus and an influential scholar in computer science. Knuth questioned the limits of data science from an ethical perspective when interviewed by the New York Times (*Roberts, S. (2018). The Yoda of Silicon Valley. The New York Times. Retrieved 25 February 2019 from*—https://www.nytimes.com/2018/12/17/science/donald-knuth-computers-algorithms-programming.html).

"I am worried that algorithms are getting too prominent in the world ... It started out that computer scientists were worried nobody was listening to us. Now I'm worried that too many people are listening."

Knuth is not alone in his concerns about how algorithms can influence our lives. Although algorithms themselves are always ethically neutral, the actions that flow from them do have consequences. We defined data science as a tool to influence reality in the *Useful Data Science* section. Algorithms can have a real impact on the world, which implies that they are subjects to ethics.

This section provides some ethical guidelines that managers can use in any discussion about whether a specific use of data is ethically justified. *Chapter 2, Good Data Science,* defined good data science as being useful, sound, and aesthetic. Perhaps we need to add a fourth aspect to this trivium and insist that data science also needs to be ethical.

The power of contemporary approaches to analyzing data can lead to adverse consequences, which means that the results of data science have moral implications. Data ethics is the last section of this book because it creates the boundary condition within which all activities should take place. This section discusses a framework for the ethical use of data and how practitioners can apply moral principles to their work.

The collection, storage and analysis of data that relates to humans needs to be undertaken ethically. This statement is almost a tautology, but the recent spate of instances where digital companies betrayed the trust of their customers suggests that there is a need for reflection on this issue. The privacy of digital consumers has been violated numerous times and some algorithms potentially harm the consumer. The ethics of data science goes beyond privacy, as the outcomes of algorithms can negatively impact our lives. Algorithms can reinforce discrimination and reduce the power of buyers in a free market (C. (2016). *Weapons of Math Destruction: How Big Data Increases Inequality and Threatens Democracy. New York: Crown*).

Ethics is a nebulous term, especially for data scientists who are more comfortable interpreting objective numbers than dealing with subjective moral reasoning. The ethics of data science is one of those problems that data science itself cannot solve. There are no algorithms that can help us in deciding whether something is ethical. Ethical issues are best resolved through contemplation and debate. Philosophers have put forward several competing models for ethical reasoning, none of which has gained anything close to universal acceptance.

The ethical perspective is closely related to the legal point of view, but they are not necessarily the same. From the fact that an action is legal, you cannot conclude that it is also ethical, and vice versa. The pace of technological change is much faster than legislative change, which means that there is a need for ethical reflection on data science. Given that the legal framework for data differs from country to country, and even between states within countries, this section only discusses the principles of ethical data science.

The ethics of gathering, storing, and interpreting information that describes the lives of people has been well developed in traditional social research. Social scientists have developed these principles in response to negative experiences with unethical research. Three crucial ethical principles that apply to data science, as per *Bryman, A., & Bell, E. (2011). Ethics in Business Research. In Business Research Methods (3rd ed.) Oxford: Oxford University Press*, are as follows:

- **Informed Consent**: In social research, all subjects must consent to their data being collected and analyzed. When we ask people to complete surveys, subjects can choose which information they provide, or abstain from providing information about themselves. The principle of informed consent ensures that participants are neither deceived nor coerced into surrendering information about their personal lives.

  Informed consent applies as much to scholarly research as it does to business operations. Recent high-profile cases with Facebook contradict this notion and suggest that the Facebook community expects that all governments, researchers, and businesses seek consent for any information they collect about people. Informed consent relies on three conditions. Firstly, the subject of the information gathering needs to be informed. Secondly, consent must be given voluntarily without undue influence. Lastly, the person consenting must have the capacity to consent, which requires them to be able to understand the consequences of opting in. Many of the ethical breaches published in the news relate to breaching either of these three conditions of informed consent.

- **Avoiding Harm in Collecting Data**: In social research, harm in collecting data includes any physical or psychological consequences for the participant, such as their development or self-esteem, inducing stress and introducing risk to career prospects or future employment. Privacy is the most significant concern regarding this principle. Most countries have well-established privacy legislation that defines how organizations deal with data. One of the most common ways to protect privacy is to anonymize data. Making data anonymous involves stripping it from personally identifying information such as names and addresses. Aggregating data is one of the methods to remove personal data. By aggregating data into groups, any link with individuals seems to be removed. However, when these aggregated sets of data are combined with other sets, the individual entries can (in principle) be decomposed. In an age of ever-increasing availability and size of data, anonymity becomes almost impossible to guarantee. A tension exists between protecting privacy and gaining societal benefits from data. (*Oppermann, I. (2017). Data Sharing Frameworks (Technical White Paper). Sydney: Australian Computer Society*).

- **Doing Justice**: Doing justice to participants implies that any analysis and interpretation of information about customers reflects their interests. Doing justice to the subjects of the analysis means algorithmic fairness. This concept expresses the risk of potential harm to people or the natural environment through the way the data is analyzed.

  Algorithmic fairness exists in two areas. Machine learning algorithms use information from the past to predict possible futures. Because of this foundation in the past, any machine learning algorithm will amplify any bias that exists within the training data. For example, a recruitment algorithm that searches for candidates on LinkedIn for an engineering job is likely to be gender-biased because of the past societal preference for male engineers.

  The second aspect of algorithmic fairness relates to an imbalance in power between the subject of data science and the organization that uses the algorithm. Online shops can use machine learning to present every visitor to their website with a different price. Algorithms can maximize the amount that customers pay for a service. Although perfectly legal, this is only possible due to an imbalance in power between the seller and the buyer.

  Algorithmic fairness is a topic of much discussion in the industry and media. The new capabilities of machine learning will require society to rethink its moral and legal frameworks as we enter previously unknown territory.

- **Don't Be Creepy:** These three principles provide a starting point for starting a discussion about ethical data science. Ethical principles, instead of values and fixed rules, are a useful tool to help clarify any potential ethical issues in a data science project.

  These three principles can be summarized into a simple principle: "Don't be creepy". When you have a data science proposal and are not sure about its ethical status, then perhaps you should ask a few friends about how they would feel about being a subject in this analysis.

References

Anderson, C. (2015). *Creating a Data-Driven Organization: Practical Advice from the Trenches*. Sebastopol, CA: O'Reilly Media Inc.

Bennett, C.M., Baird, A.A., Miller, M.B., & Wolford, G.L. (2009). Neural correlates of interspecies perspective taking in the post-mortem Atlantic Salmon: an argument for multiple comparisons correction. *NeuroImage*, 47, S125. https://doi.org/10.1016/S1053-8119(09)71202-9.

Bryman, A., & Bell, E. (2011). Ethics in Business Research. In *Business Research Methods (3rd ed.)*. Oxford: Oxford University Press.

Burkov, A. (2019). *The Hundred-Page Machine Learning Book*. LeanPub.

Caffo, B., Peng, R., & Leek, J.T. (2018). *Executive Data Science. A Guide to Training and Managing the Best Data Scientists*. LeanPub.

Carretero, S., Vuorikari, R., Punie, Y., European Commission, & Joint Research Centre. (2017). *DigComp 2.1 The Digital Competence Framework for Citizens with Eight Proficiency Levels and Examples of Use*.

Clegg, B. (2017). *Big Data: How the Information Revolution Is Transforming Our Lives.* Icon Books.

Davenport, T.H., & Patil, D.J. (2012). [Data scientist: The sexiest job of the 21st century– https://hbr.org/2012/10/data-scientist-the-sexiest-job-of-the-21st-century. *Harvard Business Review*, 90(10), 70–76.

Davis, P.J., & Hersh, R. (1990). *Descartes' Dream. The World According to Mathematics.* London: Penguin.

DeVellis, R.F. (2011). *Scale Development: Theory and Applications* (3rd ed.). SAGE Publications.

Harrower, M., & Brewer, C.A. (2003). ColorBrewer.org: An Online Tool for Selecting Color Schemes for Maps. *The Cartographic Journal*, 40(1)–https://doi.org/10.1179/0008 70403235002042).

Huff, D. (1985). *How to Lie with Statistics* (Reprint). Harmondsworth: Penguin Books.

Jaworski, B.J. (2011). On managerial relevance. _Journal of Marketing_, 75(4), 211–224– https://doi.org/10.1509/jmkg.75.4.211.

Jones, G. E. (2007). *How to Lie with Charts* (2nd ed). Santa Monica, Calif: LaPuerta.

Kelleher, J.D., & Tierney, B. (2018). *Data science.* Cambridge, Massachusetts: The MIT Press.

Lankow, J., Ritchie, J., & Crooks, R. (2012). *Infographics: The Power of Visual Storytelling.* Hoboken, N.J: John Wiley & Sons, Inc.

Lee, N., & Lings, I. (2008). *Doing Business Research: A Guide to Theory and Practice.* London: SAGE.

Lindström, M. (2010). *Buy.Ology: Truth and Lies About Why We Buy.* New York: Broadway Books.

Matejka, J., & Fitzmaurice, G. (2017). Same Stats, Different Graphs: Generating Datasets with Varied Appearance and Identical Statistics through Simulated Annealing. *In Proceedings of the 2017 CHI Conference on Human Factors in Computing Systems - CHI '17* (pp. 1290–1294). Denver, Colorado, USA: ACM Press–https://doi. org/10.1145/3025453.3025912.

McShane, S., & Travaglione, T. (2005). *Organisational Behaviour on the Pacific Rim* (Enhanced ed.). North Ryde N.S.W.: McGraw-Hill.

O'Neil, C. (2016). *Weapons of Math Destruction: How Big Data Increases Inequality and Threatens Democracy.* New York: Crown.

Oppermann, I. (2017). *Data Sharing Frameworks* (Technical White Paper). Sydney: Australian Computer Society.

Pletser, V. (2012). Does the Ishango Bone Indicate Knowledge of the Base 12? An Interpretation of a Prehistoric Discovery, the First Mathematical Tool of Humankind. Eprint—https://arxiv.org/abs/1204.1019.

Prevos, P. (2017). Lifting the 'Big Data' Veil. Creating Value through Applied Data Science. *Water E-Journal*, 2(1), 1–5—https://doi.org/10.21139/wej.2017.008.

Prevos, P. (2015). Visualizing water quality: A graphical index for drinking water system performance. In *OzWater*. Adelaide: Australian Water Association.

Prevos, P. (2012). The incompleteness theorem of performance measurement in service delivery. In *World Business Capability Congress*. Auckland: Centre for Organizational Excellence Research (COER).

Siegel, E. (2016). *Predictive Analytics: The Power to Predict Who Will Click, Buy, Lie, or Die*. Wiley.

Taylor, F.W. (1997). *The Principles of Scientific Management*. Mineola, N.Y: Dover Publications.

Tufte, E. R. (1997). Visual Explanations: Images and Quantities, Evidence and Narrative. Cheshire, Conn.: Graphics Press.

Welch, J. (2001). *Straight from the Gut*. Warmer Books.

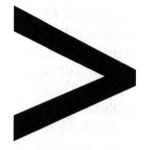

Index

About

All major keywords used in this book are captured alphabetically in this section. Each one is accompanied by the page number of where they appear.